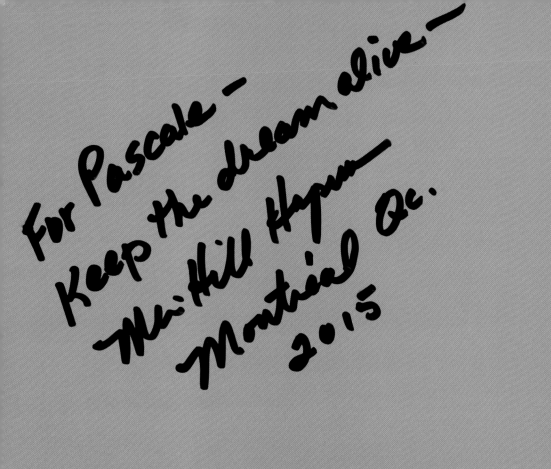

For Pascale –
Keep the dream alive –
Mei-Hill Hyman
Montréal Qc.
2015

Sea Winter Salmon

Chronicles of the St. John River

Looking south from the St. John River toward the village of the same name. The boats are in the river's estuary, with Robin's Point on the far horizon. On the right is a *goélette*, a thirty-foot schooner that displaced between twenty and fifty tons, with lateen rigging and sails. These small manoeuvrable boats sport two masts, fore and aft rigged, and were used for the offshore cod fishery all year long, safely carrying up to five crew members. These boats were the workhorses of the North Atlantic.

PHOTO: LOUIS W. HILL SR., C. 1900 – MINNESOTA HISTORICAL SOCIETY

Sea Winter Salmon

Chronicles of the St. John River

by Mari Hill Harpur

with Eileen Regan McCormack

Dedication

Louis Ernest Dérosby (1937 – 2013) —affectionately known as Coco—was a guide at Hill Camp. Coco was a thoughtful and kind gentleman who embraced old and new traditions with dignity and enthusiasm.

PHOTO: MARI HILL HARPUR, 2011 – MHH PERSONAL COLLECTION

To you, *Salmo salar*, who inspires life.

ANDO HIROSHIGE, THE LARGE FISHES, C. 1833, INGELHEIM CATALOGUE, NO. 130.

Art direction: Steve Louis, Studio Lézard
Cover illustration: Three Generations, Elizabeth Skelly, pencil and watercolour
Previous page: original watercoloured intaglio print of an Atlantic salmon-trout, created in May 1991 by Brenda Guiled at the Nova Scotia College of Art and Design printmaking studio.

Library and Archives Canada Cataloguing in Publication
Harpur, Mari Hill, author, photographer
Sea winter salmon : chronicles of the St. John River / Mari Hill Harpur; with Eileen Regan McCormack.
Includes bibliographical references.
ISBN 978-1-927535-68-4 (pbk.)
1. Hill, James J. (James Jerome), 1838-1916. 2. Hill family. 3. Atlantic salmon fisheries--Québec (Province)--Saint John River (La Côte-de-Gaspé). 4. Atlantic salmon--Québec (Province)--Saint John River (La Côte-de-Gaspé). 5. Ecology--Québec (Province)--Saint John River (La Côte-de-Gaspé). 6. Ecology--Québec (Province)--Longue-Pointe. 7. Longue-Pointe (Québec)--History. 8. Saint John River (La Côte-de-Gaspé, Québec)--History. I. McCormack, Eileen Regan, author II. Title.
FC2945.S3115H37 2015   971.4'77   C2014-906285-0

Printed and bound in Canada by Marquis.

Legal Deposit, Library and Archives Canada
et Dépôt légal, Bibliothèque et archives nationales du Québec.

Linda Leith Publishing gratefully acknowledges the support of SODEC for its publishing programme.

LINDA LEITH PUBLISHING

Linda Leith Publishing
P. O. Box 322, Victoria Station
Westmount, Quebec H3Z 2V8 Canada
www.lindaleith.com

Contents

Preface 3

Introduction 4

Chapter One   **Running the Seas** 6
     Images and Anecdotes of the North Atlantic 6
     Geography and Politics: The Seigneurial System 12
     The River, Its People, and Its Fishery (1856) 13

Chapter Two   **Looking for a River (1887 – 1900)** 18
     A Good Salmon River 18
     The Esquimaux River 22
     The Moisie River 24
     The St. John River 25
     The Chambers Family: Guides and Guardians 32

Chapter Three   **A Place of His Own** 36
     Building Hill Camp (August 1900 – June 1901) 36
     Fishermen Arriving and Surviving (1900 – 1916) 45

Chapter Four   **A Daily Rhythm (1912 – 1916)** 56

Chapter Five   **Traditions and Transitions (1901 – 1987)** 66
     A Woman's River Too 68
     The Next Generations 75
     Great-Grandchildren Go Fishing 75
     Preparing for the New Millennium 94
     Stepping Lightly into the Future 95

Chapter Six   **From Recreation to Resource Management (1989 – 2012)** 100
     The New Millennium: Centennial Observations and the Science of it All . . 102
     Yesterday, Today, Tomorrow 112
     The Last Cast 114

Appendix I   **Biographies** 118
     James J. Hill (1838 – 1916) 118
     Louis W. Hill Sr. (1872 – 1948) 119
     James J. Hill's Descendants and the Progression of Hill Camp Ownership . . 121
     The Chambers Family and a North Shore Tale 122
     Robert C. Minor (1868 – 1947) 125
     John Justin Toomey (1858 – 1942) 125
     Biologists, Guides, and Residents: Streamside Research and Beyond 126

Appendix II   **Fish Tales: Friendships and Frivolity** 127

Acknowledgements 138

Bibliography and a Note on Sources 140

Gallery 142

There are many ways a fish can speak of its journey. These two photographs show the head and tail of a wild Atlantic salmon. Notice the markings on the body. This fish has encountered an ocean net that caused extensive damage to its scales and skin.

PHOTOS: MARI HILL HARPUR, 2003 – PERSONAL COLLECTION

A carved reproduction of Louis W. Hill Sr.'s 1906 record fish, which adorns the dining room at Hill Camp. This fish had the distinction of being the largest salmon ever properly recorded on the St. John River, weighing 16.6 kg (36.5 pounds).

PHOTO: MARI HILL HARPUR, 2011 – MHH PRIVATE COLLECTION

Preface
(50° 28' N / 64° 33' W)

"To Egil Boeckmann
For we in thought of happy days shall live twice over "

This message is engraved on a silver bowl that was presented to the author's relative in 1939. The engraving includes an outline map of the St. John River.

Egil Boeckmann, James J. Hill's son-in-law, admiring his catch at Hill Camp, 1933.

If a fish could communicate with us, what tales would it tell? What does the world look like through a fish's eyes?

This is a biography of the Rivière St-Jean (hereafter referred to as the St. John River, as it was known by the region's anglophones), as well as the story of those who have frequented its shores. My family has owned the lower part of this river for over a hundred years. Included in the river's narrative is an account of its most important visitor, faithful companion, and partner: the Atlantic salmon, *Salmo salar,* the river's principal inhabitant. This is the river's story, and the salmon's story. This chronicle is about their lives together along a riverbank on the north shore of the Gulf of St. Lawrence in Canada.

∞

My great-grandfather, James J. Hill (1838 – 1916), lived through times that encompassed immense change and development, which bolstered his innate curiosity and ability to assess a situation rapidly. He was determined to be every bit a part of the world as he understood it. In sixteen of his seventy-eight years, he fished on the St. John River in Eastern Canada. In *A Moveable Feast*, Hemingway wrote, "Still, one does not forget people because they are dead." I feel that I can extend that sentiment to the fish in my great-grandfather's beloved river, as well as to all of those who have angled for them.

When we contemplate a family history, the history of a region, and that of a nation, clear and sharp images stand out. Because we are intrigued by these images, we learn to investigate them. Behind their two-dimensional features stand real people, real friends, real family, and often some strangers. The following pages hold some of the fishing narratives influenced by the St. John River, collected by my family since 1887. This is a story of that river and some of the fish and people who have been touched by its magic. If we could only unravel all of their tales, we would live another life through their eyes. We will never forget the thrill of being a part of this river's vitality.

Mari Hill Harpur
Montreal

Introduction

In the late 1890s, my great-grandfather James J. Hill began negotiations to lease and purchase the St. John River from the Dominion of Canada and the Labrador Company. As a child born in the wilderness of Ontario, he was comfortable being in remote places. In addition to being an entrepreneur and railroad pioneer, my great-grandfather was also a keen fisherman. He was an early member of the famous Restigouche Salmon Club and fished many of the best North American salmon rivers. By 1903, with negotiations completed, he owned the lower 19.3 kilometres (12 miles) of the St. John River and had obtained a long-term lease for the upper portion of that river. Thus began my family's involvement with that river, its fish, and its people.

The St. John remains a pristine watershed and an important river for generations of Atlantic wild salmon. There is no longer any netting of salmon in the river's mouth and sport fishing is controlled. Over the years, until his death in 1916, James J. Hill dedicated all of his leisure time to participate in and preserving the natural paradise of the river. In the relatively short span of his association with this river, a strong relationship was developed with the community of the village of St-Jean. This association has been perpetuated throughout the decades that followed. As the generations of salmon flowed through our camp, so have the Hill relatives. Year after year we have returned to share the splendour of spring renewal. The local community remains clearly connected to my great-grandfather's camp. Our lives and those of the local population are tightly interwoven by a shared respect for the river. To a great extent, we depend on each other to achieve our goals.

As well, my husband Doug Harpur and I have implemented an advanced scientific program of research that includes fish tagging and tracking. Catch and release is practiced extensively. We are delighted to have improved the quality of our river and we feel we have been of service to the fish in the best possible manner.

TIMELINE

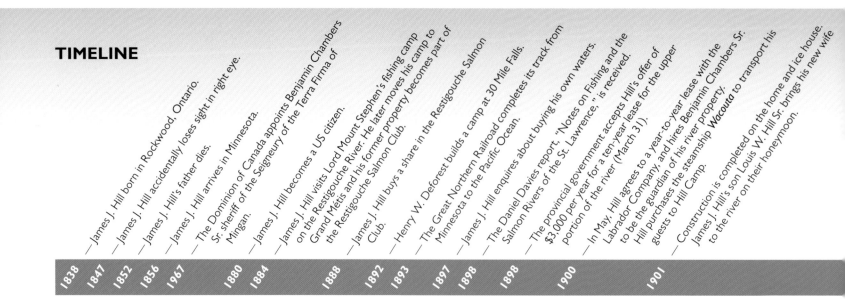

- 1838 — James J. Hill born in Rockwood, Ontario.
- 1847 — James J. Hill accidentally loses sight in right eye.
- 1852 — James J. Hill's father dies.
- 1856 — James J. Hill arrives in Minnesota.
- 1967 — The Dominion of Canada appoints Benjamin Chambers Sr. sheriff of the Seigneury of the Terra Firma of Mingan.
- 1880 — James J. Hill becomes a US citizen.
- 1884 — James J. Hill visits Lord Mount Stephen's fishing camp on the Restigouche River. He later moves his camp to Grand Métis and his former property becomes part of the Restigouche Salmon Club.
- 1888 — James J. Hill buys a share in the Restigouche Salmon Club.
- 1892 — Henry W. Deforest builds a camp at 30 Mile Falls.
- 1893 — The Great Northern Railroad completes its track from Minnesota to the Pacific Ocean.
- 1897 — James J. Hill enquires about buying his own waters.
- 1898 — The Daniel Davies report, "Notes on Fishing and the Salmon Rivers of the St. Lawrence," is received.
- 1898 — The provincial government accepts Hill's offer of $3,000 per year for a ten-year lease for the upper portion of the river (March 31).
- 1900 — In May, Hill agrees to a year-to-year lease with the Labrador Company, and hires Benjamin Chambers Sr. to be the guardian of his river property. Hill purchases the steamship *Wacouta* to transport his guests to Hill Camp.
- 1901 — Construction is completed on the home and ice house. James J. Hill's son Louis W. Hill Sr. brings his new wife to the river on their honeymoon.

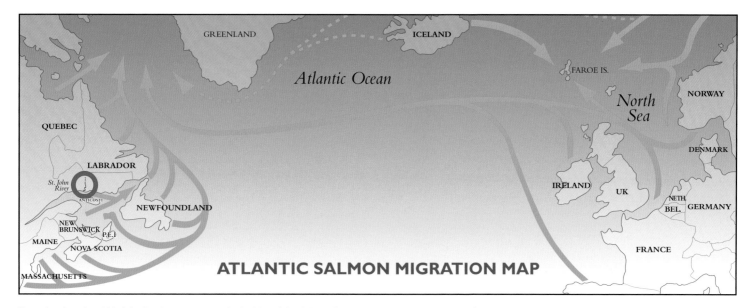

ATLANTIC SALMON MIGRATION MAP

From the rivers in which Atlantic salmon spawn on both sides of the Atlantic Ocean, they migrate to rich ocean feeding grounds where they grow quickly. The Atlantic salmon, unlike the Pacific salmon—which die after spawning—may return to the sea to repeat the migration and spawning pattern. Some Atlantic salmon only pass one winter at sea before returning, and are called grilse. Many spend two years or more at sea, and return to their home rivers as large salmon. Each period at sea is referred to as a sea winter. Tracking research conducted by the Atlantic Salmon Federation over the past decade has shown that a large number of Atlantic salmon from rivers surrounding the Gulf of St. Lawrence travel to feeding grounds near Greenland by way of the Strait of Belle Isle that separates Newfoundland and Labrador.

MAP: TOM MOFFATT, ATLANTIC SALMON FEDERATION

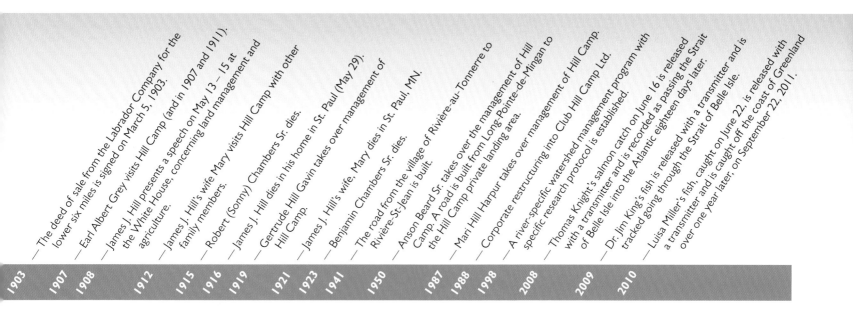

— The deed of sale from the Labrador Company for the lower six miles is signed on March 5, 1903.

— Earl Albert Grey visits Hill Camp (and in 1907 and 1911).

— James J. Hill presents a speech on May 13 – 15 at the White House, concerning land management and agriculture.

— James J. Hill's wife Mary visits Hill Camp with other family members.

— Robert (Sonny) Chambers Sr. dies.

— James J. Hill dies in his home in St. Paul (May 29).

— Gertrude Hill Gavin takes over management of Hill Camp.

— James J. Hill's wife, Mary dies in St. Paul, MN.

— Benjamin Chambers Sr. dies.

— The road from the village of Rivière-au-Tonnerre to Rivière-St-Jean is built.

— Anson Beard Sr. takes over the management of Hill Camp. A road is built from Long-Pointe-de-Mingan to the Hill Camp private landing area.

— Mari Hill Harpur takes over management of Hill Camp.

— Corporate restructuring into Club Hill Camp Ltd.

— A river-specific watershed management program with specific research protocol is established.

— Thomas Knight's salmon catch on June 16 is released with a transmitter and is recorded as passing the Strait of Belle Isle into the Atlantic eighteen days later.

— Dr. Jim King's fish is released with a transmitter and is tracked going through the Strait of Belle Isle.

— Luisa Miller's fish, caught on June 22, is released with a transmitter and is caught off the coast of Greenland over one year later, on September 22, 2011.

1903 1907 1908 1912 1915 1916 1919 1921 1923 1941 1950 1987 1988 1998 2008 2009 2010

"Precious things are to be found."

The commission granted to Jacques Cartier in 1534 has not been located, but an order from King Francis I issued in March of the same year enlightens us as to the objective of the voyage: "To discover certain islands and lands where it is said that a great quantity of gold, and other precious things, are to be found." The 1534 account suggests a second objective—the route to Asia. To those who credit Cartier, on this first voyage, with a concern for missionary work, Lionel Groulx's answer is: "Gold, the gateway to Cathay! If there is a mystique in all this, to use a word which is so debased today, it is a mystique of merchants, behind which looms a political rivalry."

This early map of North America printed by the Jesuits is dated October 7, 1763. It depicts the St. John River as an important and well-marked boundary between Labrador and territories farther west.

Chapter One

Running the Seas

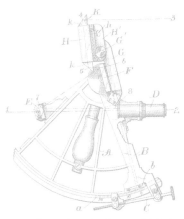

Images and Anecdotes of the North Atlantic

A river begins in two places: in geological time and in narrative time. The St. John River began to be formed when glacial ice sculpted its path during the last ice age. The river is located in an area that is known today as the Canadian Shield, Precambrian Shield, or the Laurentian Plateau. The shield's boundaries cover about half of Canada, as well as most of Greenland and part of the northern United States. It is the oldest part of the North American continental plate, with rocks dated at 3.9 billion years. It contains fossils of bacteria and algae over 2 billion years old, among the oldest on Earth. The shield is composed of metamorphic rocks and granites and is Earth's greatest area of exposed Precambrian rock. Shield areas were the first parts of Earth to be permanently elevated above sea level; accordingly, they form the cores of major continental plates (e.g. Africa, Australia, Eurasia, and North and South America). The recurring advance and retreat of the ice sheets, 1.6 million to 10,000 years ago, depressed the surface and created Hudson Bay, scraped out tens of thousands of lake basins, carried away much of the soil cover, and deposited glacial debris. The shield plateau ranges from 305 to 610 metres (1,000 – 2,000 feet) above sea level. In northern Labrador and on Baffin Island, the crustal plate has reacted to the unloading and retreat of the glacial ice by tilting so much that it rises over 1,500 metres (5,000 feet) above sea level. There are a number of mountain ranges within the shield: the Adirondacks (northeastern New York State), Superior Highlands (northern Minnesota, Wisconsin, and Michigan states), Mealy Mountain in Labrador, the Torngat Mountains in Newfoundland, and the Laurentians. The Laurentians form the Quebec portion of the Canadian Shield, particularly the area partially bordered by the Ottawa, St. Lawrence and Saguenay rivers, and encompassing the St. John River in its

entirety. It is one of the oldest mountain regions in the world. It is generally a heavily forested area with innumerable lakes and swift rivers. It is a wild and remote place. Below and above the geological surface, as King Francis suspected, there were many precious things waiting to be discovered.

Although the sea was and still is an influential presence relative to the region around the St. John River, the Laurentian Shield, with its granite bluffs dropping from the Arctic tundra to the great St. Lawrence River, was an important geological aspect of everyday life. Flowing from the rugged uplands of the Labrador peninsula, today, the St. John River tumbles toward the salt water for over 240 kilometres (150 miles) into the great and expansive St. Lawrence River. This is the highway of the river's history. This is where our story unfolds. This is where adventurers, some known and some nameless, came to explore and search for things mysterious and precious.

Who were the early people who would make their legends from this land? As myths and folktales developed, the early narratives were at first oral and then written. Through different voices and through stories and songs that have been passed down through generations, we become familiar with village life and the surrounding river settlements.

The earliest recorded visitors known to have sailed this Maritime basin appeared about 7,500 years ago and founded staggered settlements along the shore. This barren, sea-lashed coast was home to the Maritime Archaic Indians, who hunted and fished the coasts of Labrador and Newfoundland for more than two thousand years. The first evidence of the Maritime Archaic culture was discovered more than thirty years ago when James A. Tuck of the Memorial University of Newfoundland excavated fifty-six elaborate burial sites exposed during housing construction on a small promontory at Port au Choix on the Gulf of St. Lawrence, just south of the Strait of Belle Isle. This is the most educational Maritime Archaic site excavated to date. This long-term community may have been established because of the annual arrival of migrating harp seals each spring, which provided a reliable and predictable food source.

Another early culture, the Red Paint People, existed in the area. They lived in Maine and the Maritimes approximately 4,000 years ago. Their name is derived from their use of the mineral red ochre (iron oxide) in burial ceremonies. They sprinkled quantities of it on their dead and over all the gifts they placed in the graves. They are considered to be part of the Archaic Period, which ended about 3,000 years ago with the advent of the Ceramic Period. Buried between 4,400 and 3,300 BP (before present), along with the dead were tool kits containing woodworking implements for building dwellings and watercraft, finely wrought bone and ivory fishhooks, harpoons, harpoon heads, bone foreshafts, long, narrow, ground slate lances for hunting whale and walrus, and fragments of fish spears. These artifacts point to a lifestyle dependent on the deep sea. Evidence of these peoples has been traced around the northern Atlantic area, as far north as Nulliak, Newfoundland and south to the Maine border. Evidence of Red Paint settlements have been found north of Baie-Comeau in eastern Quebec. In that proximity is a place known as Pointe-des-Monts, also referred to as Pointe-des-Morts. This particular site offered up tools and numerous remains of the same early culture as in Labrador. That early group and those that followed made further settlements, recently excavated, off the coast of Labrador at a place now named L'Anse Amour. The earlier name had been known as L'Anse La Mort. These sites are common in that under certain conditions the rich red of iron oxide runs freely to the sea and colours the surrounding waters.

The Innu are descended from Algonquian-speaking hunter gatherers who were one of two Aboriginal peoples inhabiting Labrador at the time of European arrival. The major Innu communities in Labrador are Sheshatshiu on Lake Melville in central Labrador and Utshimassit (Davis Inlet) on Labrador's northern coast. Some archaeologists believe that the southern branch Maritime Archaic people may have been the distant ancestors of today's Innu. Little is understood about these early inhabitants of the area.

Following in the wake of these ocean-going peoples, other ancient vessels sailed to the area's rich fishing grounds. The skin curraghs of the early Irish, the Viking oar boats, the small *goélettes* of Brittany, and the Basque Red Bay *chalupa* brought other Maritime visitors and fishermen across the ocean.

The Vikings had occupied parts of the Arctic by about 1,000 AD. In what Leif Eriksson called Markland was one of three known settlements along the North Atlantic shore. Here the Vikings met the indigenous peoples, whom they called Skraelings, now viewed as a pejorative term that means "barbarian" or "foreigner." Where the Vikings first landed they wrote sagas describing a place of snow, flat rocks, and small trees that ran up to the ocean's edge. The Viking sailors found a "stream that glistened with salmon." We will never know all the sights sailors like Eriksson and his thirty-five men saw, but we know they dreamed of food and prosperity. Much later, many others sailed here from Europe toward religious freedom. And in the late nineteenth and early twentieth centuries, more Europeans followed. Some of these explorers and trailblazers left their marks on history, while others disappeared without a trace.

Over the next five hundred years of recorded history, sailors "discovered" trade routes along the North Atlantic seaboard. Enterprising groups established cod and whaling stations that supported small settlements that embraced local customs and interacted with the local communities. Early settlers were brave and notoriously resourceful. They represented many nationalities and interests. They protected their belongings. They fought pirates and smugglers, and occasionally they participated in their own illegal activities. Competition was fierce and frequent. The area became a busy place!

In 1497, representing His Majesty's England, John Cabot, an Italian in command of five British ships, explored as far from his mother country as modern-day Iceland. The following year, Cabot captained a fifty-ton vessel, an old trading ship called *Matthew*, and landed in North America on June 24, 1498. Over five hundred years later, this same day would mark a festival for modern Quebec's national identity: St-Jean-Baptiste Day (the feast day of Saint John the Baptist), also called Midsummer. It was a popular event in the *ancien régime* of France, as well as other European nations such as Denmark, Estonia, Finland, Latvia, Lithuania, Norway, Spain, and

Montagnais at Hill Camp in 1913, standing by the icehouse with James J. Hill's steward and the camp's cook, Richard Anderson, who managed house details on the 1913 trip, along with Robert (Bob) Minor, James J. Hill's personal assistant and steward.

PHOTO: LOUIS W. HILL SR., 1913 – MHH PERSONAL COLLECTION

Sweden. Three years after setting sail for North America, Cabot's *Matthew* was documented as having been involved in smuggling goods, specifically fish, from Ireland to England. Treachery was common in those early days.

In 1534 Jacques Cartier sailed from St-Malo, France, commissioned to search for a western passage to the Spice Islands. There were two ships under his command and Cartier himself captained the *Grande Hermine*, a sixty-ton carrack that carried thirty men. After two weeks and six days of travel, the ships arrived off the coast of Newfoundland. This quick passage was quite a remarkable feat and might have even been a record at the time for the shortest Atlantic crossing. However, upon reaching the coast, they were caught in a severe storm and blown off course. In unknown territory, they sailed along the coast for 1,500 kilometres (950 miles) and put in at a natural harbour protected by seven islands. Cartier named this area Sept-Îles. Their voyage lasted 137 days. Over the course of the next nine years, Cartier made several more visits to the New World.

Sailors intruded on this environment. They brought disease, arms, and often disrupted the local economy and political structures.

Jacques Cartier's 1534 kidnapping of two Iroquois guides, Don Agaya and Taignoagny (Chief Donnacona's sons) is one example of the extent of foreign sailors' misunderstanding of local manners and customs. They forcibly took these men and "visited" St-Malo, France, for eight months. They returned to what was then called New France on May 19, 1535. Once they were reintroduced to their people, the chief's sons refused to accompany, guide, or interpret for their captors. In 1536 Cartier kidnapped ten more Iroquois, including their chief, Donnacona. All eventually died in France. Deceit and treachery often went hand in hand with discovery. As a result, the nature of indigenous peoples in relationship with Europeans would change irrevocably.

Between 1576 and 1616, fourteen English explorers followed the Labrador coast to search for elusive water routes through the continent. In 1583 Sir Humphrey Gilbert arrived in Newfoundland and established a colony under the command of Her Majesty, thereby laying the foundation for the British Empire to claim sovereignty. In the years 1599 to 1633, Samuel de Champlain, a great sailor and cartographer, made at least twenty-seven Atlantic crossings to this North Atlantic region. Throughout the late 1600s, Basque

A Montagnais family group arrives at Hill Camp in two canoes, 1913. The group is headed to the portage above Hill Camp and then onward to their summer homes by the sea in Mingan. They had been trapping all winter and this would have been their first trip back to their summer camp in over eight months.

PHOTO: LOUIS W. HILL SR., 1913 – MHH PERSONAL COLLECTION

Montagnais Memories

As told to Doug Harpur by his father-in-law, Louis W. Hill Jr.

"What was it like here when you were a kid? What do you remember?" Doug Harpur, my husband, asked my father, Louis W. Hill Jr. in the late 1980s as they sat on the screened porch at camp.

"In the spring of the year, the Native peoples returned from their winter hunting and trapping grounds. They would come down from the north, surrounded by the smell of the wood smoke that they used to process their skins. Three days before the canoes arrived, in the spring of the year, during the ice break up, the wind had to be just right, blowing from north to south for them to start their travels. The smoky smell would permeate Hill Camp. They arrived in canoes filled to the gunnels with family, dogs, and hides. They would canoe to the pool above the house, where they would portage their belongings overland to their summer homes in Mingan. I was scared of them back then. I was so scared that I crawled into the attic and hid. There was a tiny window in the roof, and I could see there were little boys my age with their families. They stopped to visit us. They didn't stay long. They wanted to get back to Mingan."

The Montagnais depart Hill Camp in their canoe.
PHOTO: LOUIS W. HILL SR., 1913 – MHH PERSONAL COLLECTION

fishermen fished the Grand Banks and settled in Beau Bois (Bruin Islet), Newfoundland. This area was protected from the open gulf by offshore islands. The Basque settlements were small thriving villages with cod factories and whaling stations.

By 1660 the Jesuits were already established in Sept-Îles. Seventy-one years later, the first Jesuit map was published in Europe. The Jesuits made converts of the indigenous peoples who lived and hunted in an area roughly the size of Europe that stretched from present-day Newfoundland to James Bay and the Arctic. Today these people identify as Innu. They have fished and hunted in this area for centuries. In *The Moisie Salmon Club*, Edward Weeks describes an original sighting of these people spearing fish in the estuary of the St. John River in the 1800s. When Europeans learned some of the Innu's seafaring skills and were able to find their way around the oceans, their vessels, too, covered the distance through northern waters.

Perhaps the most famous and respected European navigator who explored the area was James Cook. When Cook arrived in Halifax, Nova Scotia, in 1758, the St. Lawrence River was the most important highway in the New World. At that time, Cook was thirty-two and a master officer in Britain's Royal Navy. Over the next nine years, with the use of triangulation navigation, he applied the skill of bathymetry to the eastern coastline and its key harbours. The St. John River was just one of many recordings of topographical features along the thousands of kilometres Cook recorded. He never returned to this area after 1767.

By the late 1700s, the St. Lawrence River valley was a well-known entity. The New World would fast become colonized, guided by foreign designs and interests. The early settlers—those who were lucky enough to survive—helped the new arrivals stake their claims. It would be a few centuries before this area would see any roadways, and boats remained the primary mode of transportation and communication.

Geography and Politics:
The Seigneurial System

In the surrounds of the St. John River, land ownership and management were organized under the seigneurial system: a political, economic, and social structure handed down from French law. Introduced to New France by Cardinal Richelieu in 1627, the system championed the *droit du seigneur*, the "right of the lord." This *droit* gave the landowner complete authority over the administration of the seigneurial property. This system was based on ownership championed by feudal rights and obligations and the King of France theoretically sponsored these rights and obligations. The land parcels were arranged in long strips, seigneuries, which stretched out from the banks of the St. Lawrence. This land division is still clearly visible today from the air.

In the vicinity of the St. John River in the mid-1700s, there existed two seigneuries. One was Louis Joliette's seigneury (est. 1694) which encompassed the islands of Mingan and Anticosti.

The second was named the Seigneury of the Terra Firma of Mingan. This parcel included much of the north shore of the St. Lawrence River and stretched farther north to contain the entire St. John River and its watershed. The Labrador Company would eventually purchase this entire property in 1733. The lower portion of the river was divided from the main seigneurial holding by a lease negotiated by the Labrador Company. Then, in 1903, the lower part of the St. John River was offered for sale to Canadian-American railway entrepreneur James J. Hill. The purchase agreement was signed on March 5 and by June 11, 1903, James J. Hill's Montreal lawyer F. E. Meredith (of Abbott, Campbell & Meredith) wrote that he "obtained the consent of the Government of the Province of Quebec to the sale by the Labrador Company to Mr. Hill insofar as it conveyed to him the Labrador Company's rights under lease between Her late Majesty Queen Victoria to the fisheries and fishing rights in the St. John River and the estuary of the River St. John."

The River, Its People, and Its Fishery (1856)

The reputation of the St. John River as a place for good fishing was always recognized along the coast, as well as in other East Coast centres. After the mid-1700s, the cod industry was the biggest and most profitable business in the area. It was also the most competitive. The fishing rights to areas like the St. John River, however, seemed to be in constant demand and subsequently created some confusion. In the early days, there were enough fish for all, but as the population increased so did pressure on the fishery. In monitoring the fishing industry, Dominion and provincial governments, as well as private industry, butted heads.

In 1856 Jean-Baptiste Girard and Felix Beaudin from Grande River, Gaspé, followed the cod fish by sailing a *goélette* past the estuary of the St. John River, and established a tiny fishing village on the west side of the river, Village de la Rivière St-Jean (also known as the village of St-Jean). Before long the village supported 245 inhabitants, a cod factory, and a Protestant graveyard. In 1858 the Hamilton Company established a fish factory not far from the village. That company had negotiated the lease of land for the factory directly from the Labrador Company. Seventeen years later, the Charles Robin Company from the Jersey Islands purchased the rights for this cod factory and operated it from 1875 until its closure in 1914. The factory is long gone, but the landscape is the same; this headland today is known as Robin's Point.

The intense competition for fishing rights established a feverish new bureaucracy. Among other things, the local population needed to apply for fishing licenses from the Dominion of Canada and the Province of Quebec. On March 1, 1893, Benjamin Chambers Sr., a founding resident of the village of St-Jean, applied for and was issued a fishing license to net the west bank of the river's estuary just below Robin's Point. He was allowed to catch fish on the first 1.6 kilometres (1 mile) west of the estuary of the St. John River, for a payment of twenty cents per 45 kg (100 lb) of fish caught. For that privilege, Benjamin paid the princely sum of $1.80 to the Dominion Government based on the 408 kg (900 lb) of salmon he declared he would net. On September 12, 1893, Benjamin paid an additional $1.80 to the Quebec government for a license to take fish from the west bank of the river's estuary.

Opposite page: Looking north at the area around 30 Mile Falls. These falls descend between a huge granite cleft in the Laurentian Shield, as seen on the left. The bottom of the falls marked the northern boundary of the legal fishing limit.

PHOTO: LOUIS W. HILL SR. – MHH PERSONAL COLLECTION

Two men poling along the St. John River in the 1900s. One would use a pole to ascend a river and paddles to descend. The early exploration of the east coast rivers was predominantly accomplished in canoes.

PHOTO: LOUIS W. HILL SR. – MHH PERSONAL COLLECTION

DOMINION OF CANADA.

PROVINCE OF QUEBEC.

DEPARTMENT OF MARINE AND FISHERIES.

1895.

SALMON FISHERY LICENSE.

(Issued under the Fisheries Act.)

The herein named *Benjamin Chambers* resident of *St Johns River* on payment of the sum of *$20 pr 100*, is licensed from 1st May to 31st July, 1895, as Occupant, for the purpose of carrying on *Net Fishing for Salmon*, as follows:

The first mile west of the estuary limits of the river fishing

100 fathoms bar net.
40 " wings

The granting of this License neither conveys nor implies any right or claim to its continuance beyond the period stated.

The present license requires strict conformity with the various provisions of the FISHERY LAWS now (or hereafter) in force, and to all REGULATIONS emanating from the GOVERNOR GENERAL IN COUNCIL and DIRECTIONS by FISHERY OFFICERS; in default of such compliance, the same will become void and forfeited forthwith, saving moreover the penalties imposed by law.

W. Wakeham

For Minister of Marine and Fisheries.

Countersigned and dated at *Magan* this *31st* day of *May* 1895.

Geo. S. DuBerge

Fishery Overseer

Statement.

QUANTITY OF FISH TAKEN UPON THE ABOVE STATION.

No. OF SALMON. *500 lbs – $100* VALUE.

received payment this 20th april 1895

By the time James J. Hill arrived on the scene, 154 years after the Labrador Company's purchase of the seigneury that included the lower part of the St. John River, he needed considerable help to unravel the mire of bureaucratic red tape related to the salmon fishery. Two parties in particular confounded Hill and his lawyer, Meredith, with varying details of their two leases. One lease was held by the Dominion Government for the fishing and netting rights within the river and the estuary of the St. John even though the Labrador Company had included those rights as its own to sell on Hill's purchase agreement. Regardless of what the Labrador Company thought, this first lease was actively managed by the Dominion Government. As well, despite various claims, a local group of men led by Edward Coffin had held the net fishing lease at the mouth and entrance of the river for thirty years (1874 – 1904) and had paid $400 per year for that privilege. However, the river's story started to change when Hill and Meredith entered into negotiations for the ownership of the river in 1897. By 1904, when the lease held by Coffin and his colleagues was set to expire, Hill was determined to resolve the situation. He delegated Meredith to bid up to $1,500 per year to purchase those fishing rights. Hill was awarded the lease in June of that year for a yearly amount of $875, beginning in August. The lease was for nine years and was renewed at $1,200 per year in 1912 for an additional ten years.

A receipt from the Dominion of Canada for a lease provided to Benjamin Chambers Sr. shows a payment received on September 12, 1893 for 408 kg (900 pounds) of salmon caught in that year.

The lease was with the Province of Quebec for the northern part of the river, called the "Upper Camp." This area included the upper 24 kilometres (15 miles) of government land located above the remaining part of the Labrador Company's private ownership, which had been separated in 1733. Until Hill acquired the land, the Province of Quebec had leased the property to a New York City lawyer, Henry W. Deforest, and James J. Hill subsequently took over that lease. Hill's lease on this part of the river was for a nine-year period (1900 – 1909) and was signed June 16, 1898. This was valued at $3,000 per year. The lease was rewritten on February 5, 1901 for a fourteen-year period (1901 – 1915) and was valued at $3,300 per year. The third lease was signed on November 25, 1912, and covered an eight-year period (1913 – 1921) with a value of $4,200 per year.

The seemingly simple matter of a current lease expiring and Hill applying for a new lease turned into an extended battle. Meredith said that the government's position was influenced by politics and concern for the livelihoods of the present leaseholders and local settlers in the area. In March 1904 Hill and Meredith were frustrated and anxious to clarify the situation. Finally, when in that year the lease negotiations for the estuary fishing and that of the Upper Camp and subsequent netting rights were concluded, Hill was at last in control of the St. John River. He was finally able to build fishing camps along the river and control its management. Meredith said, "In the end it was Canada's Prime Minister, Sir Wilfrid Laurier, who granted Hill the lease and the netting rights."

While there are many records of events— transactions, letters, leases signed, etc.—some of these may seem conflicting to the casual reader, and, indeed, even to me. Lacking direct observation and conversations with the affected parties makes it difficult to chronicle events as precisely as I'd have liked.

The official lease of the 1904 netting privileges at the mouth of the St. John River. The Dominion government issued this lease, which includes the rights to net fish in the sea and around the mouth of the river. Understandably, control of the fishing rights in and around the gulf was of major concern to many parties.

JAMES J. HILL PAPERS – MINNESOTA HISTORICAL SOCIETY

The granite coastline in the vicinity of the village of
Rivière-St-Jean, close to the village of Magpie.

PHOTO: MARI HILL HARPUR, 2010 – MHH PERSONAL COLLECTION

Chapter Two

Looking for a River (1887 – 1900)

A Good Salmon River

"Some rivers can only be fished by young men.
This may be called an old man's river on account of safety.
I said 'grand river.' This, the St. John truly is."

— JOHN BROWN TO DANIEL DAVIES, MARCH 9, 1898

In the years leading up to his purchase of the property on the St. John River, James J. Hill belonged to a number of private sporting clubs. Hill had enjoyed hunting and fishing his entire life, and as his railroad and business career accelerated, he found time to indulge in these pursuits (see Appendix I for a short biography of Hill). He frequently fished with his friend and partner, George Stephen (Lord Mount Stephen, 1829 – 1921), at his fishing lodge at the confluence of the Matapédia and Cascapédia rivers on the Gaspé peninsula in Quebec.

The first evidence of Hill visiting Stephen's camp dates from 1884. Stephen had a small camp where he fished with his wife and invited business associates and friends. In 1886 Stephen decided to move his camp to Grand-Métis, and his former property became part of the Restigouche Salmon Club. In 1880, the year the Restigouche Club was organized, a group of New York businessmen paid $32,000 for 647 hectares (1,600 acres) that lie chiefly on the south bank of the Restigouche, at its confluence with the Matapédia. In February 1888, Hill paid $3,750 for a share in the Restigouche Salmon Club, with a $200 initiation fee and a $350 yearly fee.

The entrance to the St. John River estuary. All of the fish in the river pass this area to reach the Gulf of St. Lawrence when they travel to the open sea to their winter feeding grounds.

PHOTO: MARI HILL HARPUR, 1989 – MHH PERSONAL COLLECTION

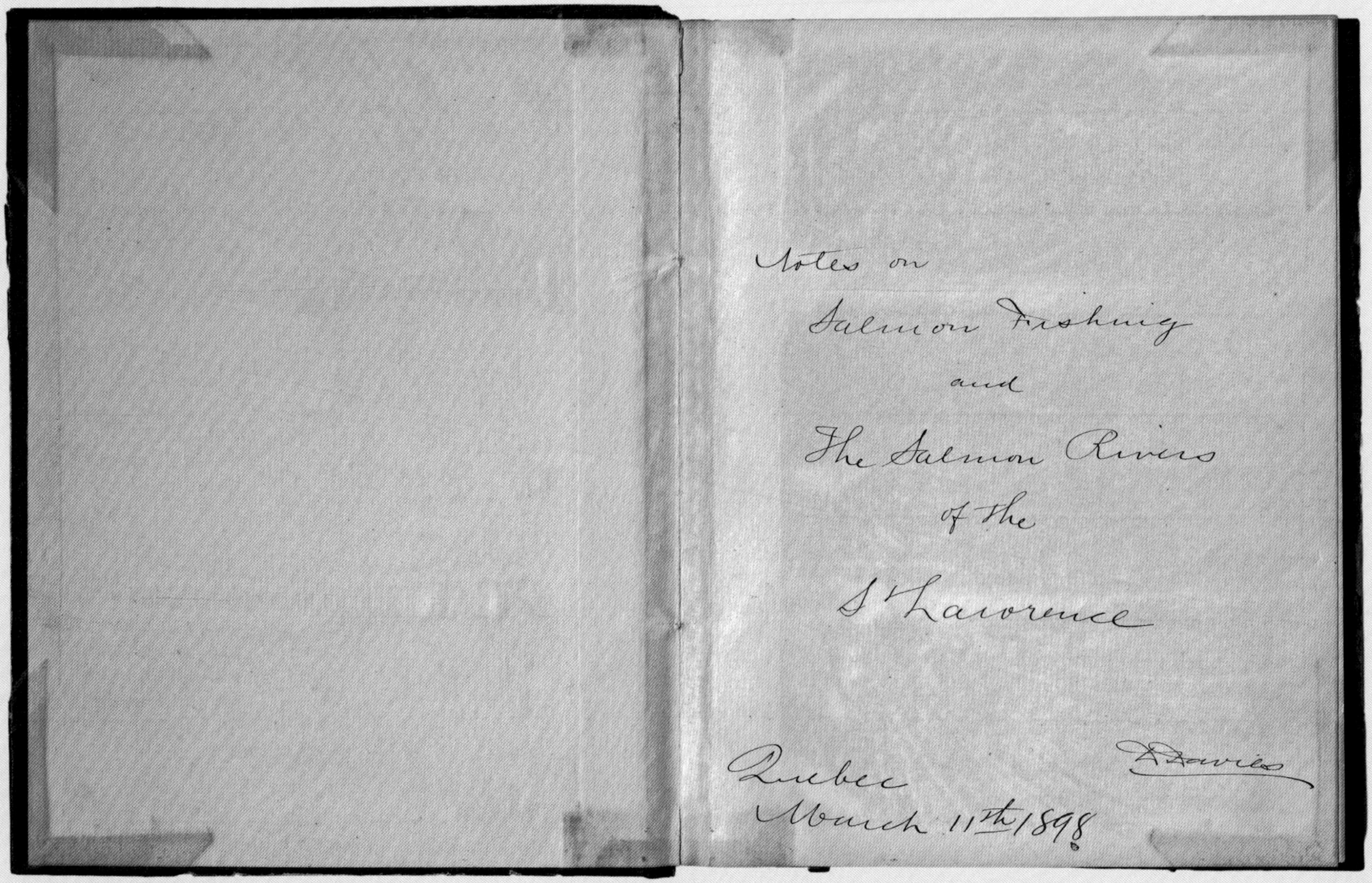

Notes on
Salmon Fishing
and
The Salmon Rivers
of the
St Lawrence

D Davies

Quebec
March 11th 1898

A reproduction of the first page of Daniel Davies's handwritten report from March 11, 1898. This report was over one hundred pages long and was submitted to James J. Hill under the title: "Notes on Salmon Fishing and The Salmon Rivers of the St. Lawrence."

ST. JOHN RIVER PAPERS – MINNESOTA HISTORICAL SOCIETY

PAGES 107 - 108 OF DANIEL DAVIES'S MARCH 11, 1898, REPORT ABOUT THE MOISIE:

Each fisherman should have two men with him to assist in the work to be done. One of these men should know the river & the haunts of the salmon, as much time would be wasted if one is not so provided. The man who acts as gaffer should be of experience in that line: otherwise you won't get the fish you hook and conquer. These men are paid about $1.00 per day. They will of course get out of you as much as they think you will withstand.

Another of James J. Hill's Canadian partners was Donald Smith (Lord Strathcona), who had a fishing camp at Rivière-du-Loup in Quebec. Other associates and friends networked the coastal areas and fished when and where they could. They were a serious group of fishermen, and they had a deep and intimate knowledge of the entire gulf area.

By 1897 it was known in Quebec that Hill was looking for a good salmon river. Finding a river, however, proved to be quite an undertaking. In his search, Hill used all of the techniques that had served him well in his business career. He engaged a small army of people in the project, including his private office staff in Minnesota, as well as attorneys and professionals influential in business and government in Montreal and Ottawa.

By early 1898 the search was put on the fast track. When the time came to choose a location for his fishing camp, Hill first turned to Canadian friends and business contacts for help. Mr. F. E. Meredith was Hill's attorney in Montreal, acting for him in the acquisition of his Quebec properties. Meredith's firm would serve Hill throughout his life, negotiating his initial river and land purchase from the Labrador Company and navigating future purchases, leases, and legal entanglements with the Dominion and Quebec governments, as well as various private concerns. Incidentally, Abbott, Campbell & Meredith were also the solicitors for the Labrador Company.

On July 17, 1898, Hill wrote John Kennedy about Daniel Davies, who was "in our service [Great Northern Railway] for some years, and he wanted a chance to visit Canada. I asked him while there to try to secure [a] good river for me, and he made a ten-year lease of the St. John's River. How he acquired it I do not know, but I assume it was largely on account of his brother, Sir Louis Davies, who is, as you know, prominent in the present Dominion Administration."

Daniel Davies relied on a few men to help him in his quest. He contacted John Brown, from Hamilton, Ontario, an entrepreneur and fisherman who lived and fished in Quebec and was one of the earliest anglers on the Moisie River. Davies also engaged a fishing guide, William Boyle from Grande-Rivière, Gaspé, Quebec, who was a seasoned canoe man and fishing guide. These men would become part of the fabric of Hill's search for what Daniel Davies called a "good river." Davies trusted the reports from these two men, and with their

help, he investigated a number of rivers to determine their present ownership or lease status, and then reviewed the existing information available from 1895. Given the number of rivers that Davies had to investigate, he gathered a remarkable amount of knowledge in a fairly short time. His first of many reports to William Toomey, Hill's private secretary, was sent in March 1898. The letters provide a wealth of information about the rivers and would prove to be invaluable source material in helping James J. Hill determine the condition of the eastern salmon rivers. As Davies wrote to Toomey:

> *I do not know what Mr. Hill's entire plan is. The instructions were for me to come down here and get a river, report upon it and wait for instructions. I cannot at this time make a selection of a given river but presuming that Mr. Hill wants some fishing the coming season and that he wants a river permanently which will grow better and better each season, I would suggest the following plan: Any of the rivers east of the Natashquan, except the Washecoota, may be leased from the Quebec Govt. Mr. L. F. Joncas, Supt of Fish & Game, will furnish a permit to fish in these rivers next season for $100 or if more than five in the party at $20 per rod and will reserve for us the privilege of making a selection from them with a view to lease or purchase.*

Davies understood the necessity of treading carefully when it came to attempting to evaluate the status of the rivers. He knew it was important to be discreet in exploring methods of fish management and protective practices. He always considered the importance of maintaining a courteous and productive relationship with the Quebec government and the local population. He included some of his observations in a letter to Toomey on March 9, 1898:

> *From what I have learned it appears that all the rivers emptying into the St Lawrence were at one time good Salmon rivers, except those having falls near the mouth which prevented the salmon ascending, the difference between them at the present time, resulting from their being cared for and protected, or left to the mercy of the poachers and netters. Those rivers which have been protected by the appointment of permanent and honest guardians …being the great Salmon rivers of today, while those not protected are valuable [only when] poachers have left them alone.*

In Davies's report, titled "Notes on Fishing and The Salmon Rivers of the St. Lawrence," he emphasized several attractions he felt were worth investigating. Davies carefully listed his conclusions on the strengths and weaknesses of the rivers Esquimaux, Kegashaka, Musquarro, Coacoacho, Etamamu, St. Augustine, Natashquan, Romaine, Moisie, and St. John. The three rivers Hill seriously considered were the Esquimaux, the Moisie, and, of course, the St. John.

The Esquimaux River

The Esquimaux River, now called the St. Paul, is the easternmost salmon river on the Quebec North Shore. It was not a well-known river at the time Hill was searching for a river because of its remote location. As an exploratory measure, Hill asked his friend Charles Bunn, who was later to accompany Hill on the 1901 fishing trip, to find out more about it. Bunn wrote Charles S. Davison, a New York attorney who had fished the Esquimaux, to send a first-hand account of his experience of the river to Hill. Davison's letter of May 22, 1901, described the river:

> *Fishing is stated to be from 40 to 60 miles above the mouth. The trip to unknown salmon fishing areas would include navigating three bays at the mouth of the Esquimaux, … then follows 8 or 10 miles [where] a boat can be rowed … then 3 miles or so of rapids one mile of which requires a portage. Next comes a bay in the river and then about ten miles of navigable water. The river takes quite a sharp bend; where there is more or less of a rapid necessitating hauling boats round the point probably for a distance of four hundred yards. After that the river is of comparatively easy navigation for about 15 miles, and above that it is alleged there is fishing …it is not believed that any one has fished with a fly for salmon in this river.*

Davison further noted that at least two camps would need to be constructed since it would take two days to reach fishing areas. He also noted that the "black flies far down this coast I have invariably found to be something which beggars description." Davison's report did not paint an enticing image.

In January 1901, Toomey began making inquiries with Hill's attorney, Meredith, discussing the tactics for concentrating on the Esquimaux River: "Our only object in leasing the St. Paul [Esquimaux] River was to use its lease as a negotiating tool to reduce the price on the St. John River." The attorney felt that when it became publicly known that Hill had acquired the Esquimaux River, the Labrador Company might lower its asking price for its section of the St. John. In February 1901 Meredith negotiated a fifteen-year lease on the Esquimaux River at $500 per year. Hill kept this river lease until 1904. As Toomey wrote in a letter to Meredith in January 1904: "You will remember that our only object in leasing the St. Paul River was to have a salmon river in case we could not secure the St. John River on reasonable terms."

On July 3, 1902, Hill's wife Mary reported in her diary: "A telegram from Papa; he will leave St. Johns [sic] River for Esquimaux River Sunday and expects to be in New York on the 12th."

So it seems Hill may have gone to the Esquimaux but certainly not to fish, as further reports indicate. William and Felix Boyle, the Gaspé canoe men employed by Hill, also went to the river to report on the conditions. William Boyle wrote that they did not catch any salmon, and they did not even see any jump! It took two to three days to get to where the salmon were thought to be, and he wrote that they had found many seals below the third falls, which "must have been after some kind of fish."

In 1903 Toomey made arrangements for Charles Bunn to make another trip to the Esquimaux River. He arrived at the river on June 20 and reported to Hill that he did not see a salmon above the nets at the mouth of the river. He went up 72 kilometres (45 miles); above that point he felt it was too dangerous. "Neither ourselves nor our guides during the whole time [June 20 – July 10] saw a fish. We rose none, none jumped and none could be discovered in the water while canoeing over the pools." Bunn seemed to feel the thousands of seals in the river had something to do with the scarcity of fish, and he quoted Charles Davison: "One seal in a pool will clean out a great number of fish. If there is a seal colony in the river I am afraid it will be very doubtful as to your getting much of any sport."

The coastline at the village of Natashquan with 150-year-old cod sheds, *Les Galets.*
PHOTO: MARI HILL HARPUR, 1995 – MHH PERSONAL COLLECTION

Hill decided, *"there is absolutely no rod fishing for salmon in the Esquimaux and it would be a waste of time to go there for that purpose."*

After reviewing all these reports, Hill decided that there was "absolutely no rod fishing for salmon in the Esquimaux and it would be a waste of time to go there for that purpose." Therefore, in August 1903, Toomey wrote Meredith that Hill wanted to give up the lease on the Esquimaux River.

The Moisie River

The Moisie River, 142 kilometres (87 miles) west of the St. John River, was the other river in which Hill expressed a particular interest.

Page twenty-one of Daniel Davies's March 11, 1898 report about the Moisie River reads:

> Spoken very highly of by every fisherman I have met. J Brown caught 202 Salmon in one season (16 days I think he said). Has been bought by Vesy Boswell a brewer of Quebec, from Alex Frazer on terms which guarantee Boswell a three years lease but gives Frazer the privilege of redemption at any time. I saw Frazer about this and he says that if a better offer were made to him than the amount paid by Boswell, before he would be bound to submit it to the latter and he would undoubtedly make up the difference so that there would be no use in attempting it. Boswell has four other gentlemen associated with him, one of them being Edson Fitch, another a Mr. Chas. Hope of Montreal. J.B. thinks Andrew Allan is one of them. They have divided the property into five portions.

The report continues:

> I had a talk with Mr. Frazer who was more communicative. He says that Boswell has a deed outright to the property for a consideration of $25,000.00 and that there is a side agreement by which Frazer is permitted to redeem the property at any time within three years. In case Frazer obtains a better offer than $25,000.00 he would have to submit it to Boswell before accepting and in any case Boswell would have the fishing rights for three years 1898, 1899, 1900. The interest on this money is offset by the rental. As there is a possibility that Mr. Hill may negotiate with Fitch for the unapportioned share, I thought it would

> be best to let the matter rest. The old gentleman (Frazer) states that he would set a price upon it, the idea being that we could state if we would give that much when he would submit to Boswell.

On July 29, 1898, Davies informed Hill, "The asking price for the Moisie is $100,000. Mr. Frazer, the owner of the Moisie and many other Quebec rivers, has the river leased to an American group until January 1, 1901, and they would get first chance to purchase it when their lease is up."

Hill began negotiations with Frazer for the fishing rights and property on the Moisie in July 1900, but by December they were discontinued. On Frazer's side there were myriad issues; he had a $25,000 mortgage owing to Mr. Boswell, and in the end it seemed that Frazer did not own the fishing rights, so Hill would have to lease those from the government. The upshot of it all was Hill might have to pay $25,000 to Boswell to settle the debt, as well as $30,000 to Frazer. The government was putting out a price of $22,000 for the purchase; however, that was subject to approval, which was by no means a given. It all seemed very tentative, and a telegram Hill sent to John Toomey in Montreal, on December 28, 1900, ended the matter. "Drop all negotiations relative to Moisie and give your whole attention to St. John for the present."

Edson Fitch (who owned 1.5 shares of the five shares of the Moisie Fishing Club as well as the entirety of the Romaine River) was another of Hill's fishing contacts and an American businessman who established the Edson Fitch Company in 1867, which manufactured match splints and blocks near Quebec City. On July 21, 1904, Fitch wrote Hill:

> Some years ago I know that you were anxious to get some fishing on the Moisie River. Perhaps you would like to get an interest there now. My friend Mr. Boswell and myself have been contesting Mr. Adams' right to fish there, and have got a judgment against him from which he has appealed, and the appealed case comes off in October. We feel perfectly certain that we shall win the case. There is room for five rods and we feel disposed to take in three with us. Of course we could do nothing …until the appeal is over.

Hill replied to Fitch on August 8 of that year, "I am well off for fishing. Some years ago I looked up the Moisie and found Mr. Boswell and yourself were interested, and so dropped the matter entirely." So ended the Moisie River saga.

The St. John River

The earliest record of the river, from a 1871 book by Napoleon Comeau in *Life and Sport on the North Shore of the Lower St. Lawrence and Gulf*, informs us that during a twenty-six-day period (June 23 – July 18, 1871), five fly fishermen from Montreal and New York caught 416 salmon on the St. John River, a total weight of 2,157 kg (4,755 lbs). The largest fish caught was 11.8 kg (26 lbs). This was a record at the time on the St. John.

On March 17, 1898, Davies sent a letter to Toomey describing the St. John River in detail: "This may be rated as one of the first class rivers; the exception to be taken to it consisting in the fact that the salmon are not large. Mr. J. (John) Brown speaks very highly of the river …It will accommodate any number of rods and will undoubtedly be taken by some American club who can pay the price unless secured before long."

The letter goes on to give the history of the ownership of the river by the Labrador Company, the lawsuit whereby the Quebec government took over partial ownership, and the lessee of the river at that time, Henry W. Deforest of New York City. One of the strong points in favour of the St. John was that Deforest had carefully guarded and improved the river for years. John Brown said, "if the river had not been guarded it would be no better than dozens of other played-out rivers."

In conclusion to his report, Davies made two recommendations. Either Hill should obtain a permit or a lease for one year on a number of rivers before he made his decision to purchase, or he should go ahead and lease the St. John River. Philip Schuyler and

George Pollock, also from New York City, had an arrangement with Deforest for the upper 45 kilometres (28 miles) of the river as well as some of the lower sections. This lease covered the period from January 1, 1890, to December 31, 1898.

James J. Hill's lease for the upper portion of the St. John River, owned by the Province of Quebec. It covers the area bought by James J. Hill from the Labrador Company's ownership, as well as the area that extends to the upper limits of the fishing area at the 30 Mile Falls. This document was dated and signed June 16, 1898..

Davies continued:

A gentleman named Denniston [a fellow fisherman and friend of John Brown's], caught 183 Salmon in this river in 16 days …The harbor and surroundings and the scenery are magnificent—in fact as Brown says ideal—just such a place as you would have made to order—lovely sandy beach, grand bathing. Chambers [Benjamin Chambers Sr.], the agent of the H. B. Co. at the mouth of the river is a fine fellow, willing to do everything in his power to make matters pleasant, knows the river, and says it is remarkable from every standpoint: caribou, hunting, good guides, telegraph office. In fact, as nearly as I can judge, what is wanted, but the price!

On March 21, 1898, Toomey wrote to Davies that Hill had made a decision to lease the government's upper portion of the St. John River. The ensuing negotiations for the river were long and difficult. It was uncertain whether any agreement could be reached regarding the government's upper 48 kilometres (28 miles) of the river, or with the Labrador Company's lower 19 kilometres (12 miles). Would the negotiations result in ownership?

On March 31, 1898, the provincial government accepted Hill's offer of $3,000 per year for a ten-year lease for the upper portion of the river. Hill and Davies now needed to concentrate on furthering the negotiations with the Labrador Company for the lower section of the river.

On May 14 William Toomey wrote to his brother, John, who was still in Quebec City, that he had sent the draft document to the Labrador Company:

I beg to say that in order to save time I think it would be well for you to call on Messrs. Richard B. Angus [Canadian Pacific Railway], Thomas Shaughnessy [Canadian Pacific Railway], Sir Edward Clouston [Bank of Montreal], John Turnbull and Sir William Van Horne [Canadian Pacific Railway] if he is in Montreal, on your return journey, and, at least, ascertain what the prospects are, if any, of Mr. Hill's purchasing the St. John's River outright from the Government. Some of these gentlemen may be willing to take the matter in hand, and, if not, perhaps they are in a position to say who would be the proper party to approach; in short; how should Mr. Hill or his representatives proceed in order to bring about the desired result? I am very glad we have all of the river for this year, which will give us more time to work on the matter.

In May 1900, just prior to his first trip to the river, Hill agreed to a year-to-year lease with the Labrador Company. He paid the company $1,000 for the year 1900. Finally, after extended negotiations, Hill was able to purchase the lower 19 kilometres (12 miles) for $50,000 on March 5, 1903. As mentioned above, it was not until 1904 that Hill was able to negotiate the purchase of the netting privileges at the mouth of the river. Having acquired the remnants of the Seigneury of the Terra Firma of Mingan from the Labrador Company, and with the approval of the Privy Council, Hill now owned his own waters and could begin creating his fishing camp.

According to Brown, the mouth of the St. John River is almost 0.8 kilometres (0.5 miles) wide. Its width measures from 91 to 160 metres (100 to 175 yards) across up to the 48 kilometres (30 miles) mark. This stretch, from the mouth to "Big Falls" (sometimes also called 30 Mile Falls), at the thirty-mile mark, is considered the river's fishing limit. Within this stretch there are a number of rapids. The current varies, however, and runs from 8 to 32 kilometres (5 to 20 miles) per hour. At the mouth, there is a harbour for vessels drawing 1.8 metres (6 feet) of water or less above the first 8 to 10 kilometres (5 to 6 miles) where the tide ends. Further navigation of the river was accomplished with canoes. For much of this distance upstream, men poled the canoes. Today, most guides use 9.9-horsepower motors on the backs of their canoes instead of the traditional poles.

The government ownership, Upper Camp, is shown on John Brown's map (see page 28). The previous lessee, Henry W. Deforest, built his house at this location, close to "Big Falls," in 1892. Toomey described the Deforest house: "It is well preserved. The location appears to be a good one. This building occupies about 50 x 30 feet of ground space; it is entirely covered with shingles, and the whole inside is sheeted with pine. The house contains four bedrooms, each with two entrances (one from the inside and the other from the outside), and a large dining room, two entrances, with a large open fire place …There is a separate cook house and outhouses." Eventually, the house washed away during a flood in the spring of 1906.

The Chambers house in the village of St-Jean was seen as a beacon from the St. Lawrence River, especially when the flag was flying. During the early days, this house was used as a post and telegraph office and was located within sight of Robin's Point and the village store.

Photo: Louis W. Hill Sr. – MHH Personal Collection

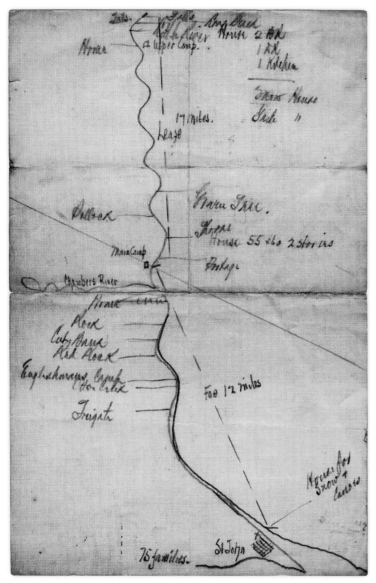

John Brown produced this drawing of the St. John River in 1889 for James J. Hill. Brown was an avid fisherman from Quebec who travelled extensively around the Maritimes. He fished regularly on the Moisie River, and since that river is so close in proximity to the St. John, we must assume that he visited both rivers often.

John Brown drew the locations of the various buildings situated on the St. John River property for James J. Hill. This image was presented to Hill before his first fishing trip to the river in the summer of 1900. That summer, Hill's secretary, John Toomey travelled to the river in advance of Hill to better understand the conditions governing the salmon fishing and to discover the state and inventory of Hill's newly acquired property. Toomey would have gathered information from a variety of sources and would have been completely familiar with the reports and letters of John Brown.

The second house, Pollock Camp, at the lower camp, was where Hill would eventually build his own log house. George Pollock's house provided the materials needed for Hill and his men to build a cookhouse and guide camp. This house was close to a high bank that was in danger of eroding, necessitating moving the house location when Hill came to build. Toomey reported: "The house is plainly constructed, the entire sheeting being covered outside with shingles …no inside finish. It occupies about 25 x 28 feet of ground, and is divided into two bedrooms and one dining room, with a large fireplace. There is a detached kitchen and a bunk house for boatmen."

As for the condition of the fishing, in a letter from Benjamin Chambers to John Brown on May 8, 1898, Chambers stated that in 1896 about 186 salmon were caught on one rod, while in 1897, a poor year with a late start, only 115 salmon were caught by two rods. Toomey also recorded the catch by Pollock and his former lease partner Schuyler, who spent two weeks at the river and caught 125 salmon with two rods in 1899. However, he added: "These gentlemen did not apply themselves closely and the general trend of information would indicate that there is room for a large party to fish and with good success on this river."

John Brown had the last word on what Hill could expect when he came to the St. John River. In a letter to Daniel Davies dated July 24, 1898, Brown wrote that he had been fishing with Benjamin Chambers in 1868 and caught fish as far up as the falls until as late as August 1. He continued to praise the river:

It is ahead of Moisie or any other river upon this coast and a peculiar change has taken place. The objection and the only one I ever had to the river was that the fish were small. That they were and, to one accustomed to the large salmon of the Moisie, this was something I could not overcome. But a mysterious change has taken place and the cause cannot be given. The fish are now ponderous fellows and I am informed their average will exceed 20 pounds. The community is industrious and respectable. The land at the mouth (where the village is located) is rich and will grow anything. There are two traders in the summer … where anything can be had in the way of coarse supplies the camp may run short of. Mr. Hill may congratulate himself on having secured the finest thing in the way of a salmon river.

But before he could consider himself ready to fish the river, James J. Hill still required help. He needed guardians who would be on the river year round. He found these in the Chambers family, longtime residents of the village of St-Jean.

The original deed of sale signed March 5, 1903 as prepared by the Labrador Company Ltd., represented by President George A. Drummond, and presented to James J. Hill, who was represented by R.S. Angus, attorney, and E.W.H. Phillips, NP, and registered in Saguenay for $50,000.00. On March 18, 1903 (Document 935), the lower portion of the St. John River, in the county of Saguenay, had registered a title on land from Telegraph Island north for 19 kilometres (12 miles), including land within 61 metres (200 feet) of high tide, as well as the fishing rights and other privileges.

St. John River Papers – Minnesota Historical Society

BEFORE ME, Edward W.H. Phillips, the undersigned Notary Public for the Province of Quebec in the Dominion of Canada, practising in the City of Montreal, in said Province.

CAME AND APPEARED.

THE LABRADOR COMPANY, a body corporate having its head office in the City of Montreal, hereinacting and represented by the Honourable George A. Drummond, the President thereof, hereto duly authorized by Resolution of the Directors of said Company, dated the Second day of February last (1903), a copy whereof is hereto attached marked "A" and duly signed and identified.

The said Company being hereinafter called the "Vendors".

Who acknowledged and confessed to have sold and conveyed with legal warranty except as hereinafter mentioned,-

UNTO JAMES J. HILL of the City of St. Paul in the State of Minnesota, one of the United States of America, Capitalist, hereinacting and represented by Richard B. Angus of Montreal aforesaid, Capitalist, his Attorney duly constituted under Power of Attorney executed before witnesses at St. Paul aforesaid on the Twenty fifth day of February last (1903), proved by Affidavit before His Majesty's Consul, and hereto attached marked "B" and duly signed and identified.

The said James J. Hill being hereinafter called the "Purchaser", and hereto present and accepting, the following property, to wit,-

DESCRIPTION.

(a) A strip of land bordering on the St. John River in the County of Saguenay in the Province of Quebec, said strip beginning at a line projected across and at right angles to the course of said river, at, but not touching, the upper end of the island known as Telegraph Island in the said river, and extending to the boundary on the North between the property of the Vendors and the

The Deforest house was the base for fishing at 30 Mile Falls.

Guides at Pollock Camp holding nine fish.

Left: The pool at the bottom of 30 Mile Falls is one of the most productive pools on the St. John River. It fishes quite late in the season because of its depth and distance from the sea. Once the *Salmo salar* enter the river's freshwater system and begin making their way upriver to spawn, they do not eat. Even so, they must perform fantastic athletic tasks as they manoeuvre up the incline of the falls, an elevation of approximately 5 metres (15 feet). The salmon jump up the incline, from one still area to another, until they are finally above the rushing water. From there they advance to the upper reaches of the river to spawn.

The Chambers Family: Guides and Guardians

Benjamin Chambers Sr. was born in 1839 in Brighton, England. He was a sailor, and like many before him, he crossed the ocean in search of a new life. He first settled in Grande-Rivière on the Gaspé peninsula, Quebec, and ten years after the founding of the village of St-Jean, Benjamin Chambers Sr., who was then twenty-seven years old, sailed from the south shore to the north shore to settle in that village with his wife, Mari-Ann (née Youth), and eleven children.

In 1867, the same year as Canadian Confederation, Benjamin Chambers Sr. became the sheriff of the Seigneury of the Terra Firma of Mingan. After the transfer of the Seigneury to the Labrador

Company, he was engaged to patrol and guard the company's property, which included an extraordinary amount of land as well as the St. John River. Chambers was employed as a boatman and a guardian for that company for thirty-three years. The Chambers family also worked for the Robin Company stores and conducted business on that company's behalf until it closed in 1914.

Circumstance placed Benjamin Chambers in a position of authority. By 1893 his family's familiarity with the neighbourhood was well established. Consequently, it was no surprise that John Brown introduced the Chambers family to James J. Hill. The Chambers family would become the guardians for the two St. John River fishing camps—one built and one leased. On Brown's recommendation, and following the letters Brown had received from Chambers, Hill retained Benjamin Chambers as the guardian of his new property with a salary of $80 per year, and Chambers hoped that Hill would extend employment to others in his family, as well.

In May 1898 Benjamin Chambers wrote to Brown, presumably in reply to a letter received:

> Glad to learn that the River is about to change hands. I wish that you would please do your best for Mr. Hill to take all my boys, there are four of them, all good canoe men and know the River well. It is hard to see strange men coming from Gaspé on this River and have boys that were … brought up on the River all their life. So I hope you will do your best for me. At the same time should be glad to have you through the summer if you wish to come …I think that Mrs. Chambers will try and make you comfortable. Hope to hear from you later on.

An early photo of the Chambers family home in the village of St-Jean. Several family members are standing on the porch.

PHOTO: LOUIS W. HILL SR. – MINNESOTA HISTORICAL SOCIETY

Because James J. Hill always required more guides and canoe men than the local village could supply, he hired canoe men from Grande-Rivière, on the south shore of the St. Lawrence River. William Boyle, as the leader of this group, was responsible for hiring and maintaining discipline among these men. They were generally employed for thirty days, at $1.75 per day, except for Boyle, who was paid $2 per day as their representative. They received their pay at the break-up of camp before their return voyage. Despite efforts to maintain camp harmony, there developed a constant friction between the local guides and the imported ones, to the extent that the "Gaspé men" had separate living arrangements at the river. To this day, the place where the Gaspé men stayed is called Englishmen Pool (le camp des Anglais).

On May 18, 1900, John Toomey wrote: "Mr. Benjamin Chambers who has been guardian of the river in the past appeared to be the only one in the vicinity qualified for the position and I arranged for him to continue in the position this year."

The relationship between Chambers and Hill was long and rich. In the early years, Benjamin Chambers Sr. ran the camp, until his son Sonny (Robert) took over. The Chambers ensured that the Hill Camp's cogs were well oiled, and so operations ran smoothly for Hill and his guests from the first season in 1900 until Hill's final visit in 1915.

After the death of James J. Hill, Louis Hill Sr. wrote to his siblings on February 11, 1919: "Those local people are very poor and need all the help they can get." The Hill presence substantially contributed to the local economy. Sonny Chambers, thus, had slim need to be concerned about his livelihood or that of his family. Hill's ownership of the lower part of the St. John River guaranteed Sonny's wages for the guardianship and ongoing maintenance of James J. Hill's camp and the leased upper camp. Sonny was the camp's supervisor and organized the local people. He successfully managed to calm the competition between the two groups of guides: the "imported" Gaspé men and the locals.

When the Chambers family took on the responsibility of guardianship, the stage was set for James J. Hill's operation to begin shaping his fishing camp. Mr. Deforest's lease on the upper river would soon expire, and after what seemed like years of accumulating information and favours among various entities, James J. Hill was poised to go fishing.

The original agreement of employment between the Labrador Company and Benjamin Chambers Sr.

Four men, three from the Chambers family, stand before the small log building that served as the original icehouse built by Robert (Sonny) Chambers in 1901. *Left to right:* Sonny Chambers, Wallace Chambers, John Chambers, and Joe Paquet.

The relationship between the Chambers family, the Innu, and Hill Camp has persisted
for over a century. The Innu are neighbours who live in the settlement of Mingan just
east of the St. John River. Pierre Piétacho, left, is seated next to his father Philippe on the
Hill Camp porch. Jean stands behind them, and Jean's father Pierre is on Philippe's lap.

Chapter Three

A Place of His Own

Building Hill Camp (August 1900 – June 18, 1901)

> *"He [James J. Hill] wanted to procure a river where he and the members of his family, or any friend that he might see fit to invite to join the family, could be together and free from coming in contact with other parties fishing in the same stream. If he did not feel that he particularly wanted a river all to himself, he would certainly be only too glad to make the arrangement suggested in your communication."*
>
> —WILLIAM TOOMEY, IN REPLY TO A 1899 LETTER FROM PHILIP SCHUYLER

Hill was fifty-nine years old when the negotiations for the river concluded in 1898. He would come to the St. John River every salmon-fishing season for the next sixteen years. As John Toomey wrote to Arthur Gagnon, a Canadian hunting and fishing inspector, on February 23, 1917: "He was always there for the first of the season …and this was the only vacation that Mr. Hill indulged in."

When Hill arrived at the river in July 1900, his new log house at the lower camp was not yet constructed. Hill chose the architect James Brodie, with whom he had worked designing buildings for the Great Northern Railway. The plans had been drawn and construction details worked out to begin building in August of that year.

Hill and his party made the Pollock site their main camp and used the Deforest house when they fished the pools near the upper falls. A September inventory for that first year shows that both the Deforest and Pollock houses were fully supplied with furniture, kitchen utensils, dishes, bedding, towels, and linens.

The Hill Camp homestead photographed during the first year of construction, 1900 – 1901, from the east side of the river, showing a canoe with two guides poling mid-river. Pollock Camp is the house at the right

PHOTO: LOUIS W. HILL SR. – MINNESOTA HISTORICAL SOCIETY

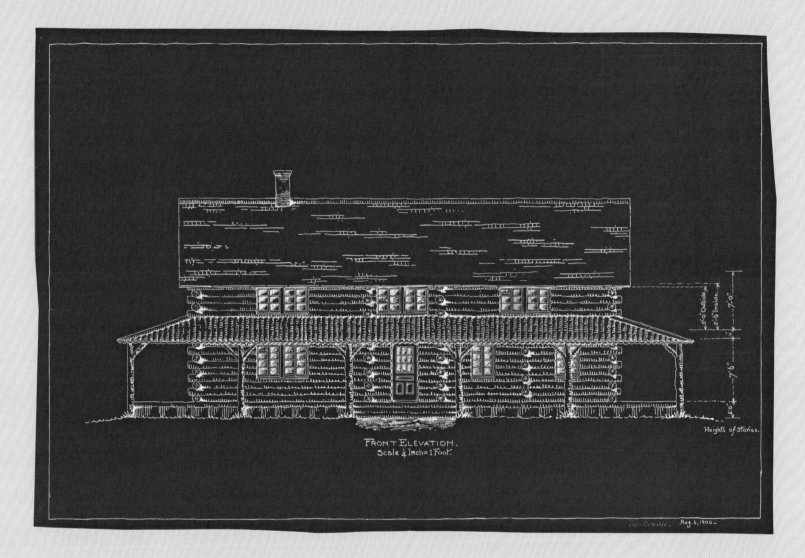

FRONT ELEVATION.
Scale ¼ Inch = 1 Foot.

Heights of Stories.

James Brodie produced this blueprint plan of the Hill Camp
house for James J. Hill. Brodie was the principal architect
for Hill's Minnesota-based business, the Great Northern
Railway. Brodie designed railway depots and office buildings
for the railroad along its extensive network in the American
northwest. He also designed and supervised construction for
Hill's homes in St. Paul, Minnesota.

MINNESOTA HISTORICAL SOCIETY

Constructing a large house in a remote area was an ambitious, labour-intensive, time-consuming project. Not only was the procurement of building materials and supplies a challenge, but hiring labourers and skilled tradesmen for the construction required investigation, organization, and fairly extensive travel arrangements. Many of the workers came from as far away as Quebec City. The winter was long, which meant the construction season was short. Hill's staff from Minnesota made on-site visits, while the local supervisor, Benjamin Chambers, monitored and reported regularly on the progress, or, unfortunately, sometimes on the lack of progress. From August to early November 1900, letters and telegrams were sent out daily, detailing instructions and relaying questions and concerns over costs and delays. Hill wanted the house completed that fall; however, from a close perusal of the activities involved, that was almost an impossible task. That the entire project moved along as quickly as it did was undoubtedly due to the fact that Hill's secretaries, the brothers William and John Toomey, kept everyone's feet to the fire and at various times cajoled and at other times threatened the people in charge of the project.

During the winter of 1900 – 1901, Hill's staff, both in Minnesota and in Quebec, busied themselves with keeping tabs on supplies being sent to Chambers so that construction of the house could resume as soon as the river ice broke up the following spring. Sonny Chambers was busy as well. He procured the materials and oversaw the construction of the icehouse, which was to be filled with snow and used to store the killed fish. He also supervised the building of a canoe storage house and wharf access built at the mouth of the river in the village of St-Jean, and he cleared a triangular piece of ground just above the new house in order to open up the view.

Construction of the new log house at Pollock Camp began immediately after Hill and his party left the river. When the house was finished, the camp would take on an appearance somewhat similar to what it is today. Rising from the river are two terraces or levels of bank. The new house was built on the higher level, set back about nine feet (2.7 metres). The Pollock house was torn down and some of the materials used in the new house. The existing two cabins were to be used by guides and canoe men.

On October 13, 1900, Toomey sent J.S. Probst from the Minnesota office to the campsite to report on the progress of the construction. Probst travelled through Quebec City and arrived at the river on October 15, bringing with him eight additional carpenters. Toomey had instructed him to judge whether or not the house could be completed before winter. That deadline would have required finishing the task in the two weeks remaining before cold weather arrived—not a likely scenario.

The final report for the year came to Toomey from Probst in November, detailing the construction progress to October 27. On that date the work was suspended for the season, "the Quebec carpenters [are] refusing to start on porch or inside work." The roof was completed, and the chimney and all window and door openings were covered until work could resume in the spring. When the conditions are taken into account, it is quite a feat that the house was as far along as it was after a two-month period. Probst, in his report, reminded Toomey that the materials used were spruce logs ranging from 7.6 metres (25 feet) long and 25 centimetres (10 inches) in diameter, to 4.6 metres (15 feet) long and 20 centimetres (8 inches) in diameter. The balsam logs used for the porch roof were also 7.6 metres (25 feet) long. He wrote of the difficulty of locating, cutting and transporting more than 4,876.8 linear metres (16,000 feet) of logs to the building site:

> Great difficulty was experienced in finding the required number of suitable logs; they were found, scattered here and there, from three to four miles up the river, and when cut had to be carried to the river and floated down to where they were wanted.

> The work of construction was necessarily slow on account of the great weight of the material that had to be handled. The heavy, wet logs had to be hauled up the two terraces from the river (one ox doing the work) and then had to be hoisted up by hand, no pulleys or other appliances being available; it took 8 to 10 men to handle one log.

At the end of his report, Probst seemed hopeful that the house would be completed by June 1, 1901, and ready for Hill and his guests' second trip to the river. However, he also wrote of the things that had to happen to make that work:

> The main problem seemed to be getting a sufficient number of workmen …to finish the work that is left, viz: the porch and all inside work will take twelve good men at least six

The hauntingly bleak shore, showing the harbour in which a small white boat is anchored. This cove is located about 20 kilometres (12.4 miles) east of the St. John River.

PHOTO: MARI HILL HARPUR, 1995 — MHH PERSONAL COLLECTION

weeks; it is difficult to get men up the river before the end of April. [Probst hoped to hire a head carpenter and crew that live "along the Coast."] These men could reach the house by dog teams at the beginning of April and being hardy men, used to the climate, they could start at that time without trouble. Chambers has left a stock of provisions at the old Pollock house and will send a cook up as soon as he is needed.

April 17, 1901 found Probst back in Montreal to oversee every aspect of the push to get the house finished by June 1. On April 29, he wired Toomey, "Marie Josephine sailed this morning at six with twenty-four workmen and all our freight." Unfortunately Probst was ill and had to stay behind, so Toomey immediately sent another employee, F.L. Pattison,

Top: On the construction site, a tent was erected as a basic shelter from the elements. This photograph was taken looking south.

Bottom: The main fireplace, made of river stones, during construction. Around the fireplace lies the timber used to build the house.

Top: The main roof of the house with tall, straight, black spruce trees on the horizon. These slow-growing trees were recognized for their strength and straight form and were sought after as masts for large sailing vessels. Black spruce was used in the making of the camp's log home.

Bottom: The finished log house looking upriver (north), with the porch on the south side.

out from Minnesota to oversee the work. He arrived at the river on May 16 and did not leave until June 12, having stayed a few days after the workmen left to make sure everything—including clean dry beds—was ready for Hill. No detail was overlooked, as is shown by the wire Pattison sent to William Toomey on June 14: "No combs or brushes here."

On June 15, Toomey sent a wire to his brother John, who was with Hill on his private railroad car, the A–18, on the way to Montreal: "You had better purchase and take down toilet soap, combs, brushes and one large tin foot bath for house."

It was an amazing accomplishment that the house had taken just under a year to complete. Over the course of six weeks that spring, the house was fully stocked, furnished, and ready for the guests. After all, obstacles regarding steamer accidents, shipping errors, missing supplies, unacceptable supplies, never-received supplies, and illness were all very difficult things to deal with, especially in a remote location. But the house was indeed finished and had the appearance of a fine building.

The two-storey structure had four bedrooms on the second floor, and a sitting room, dining room, kitchen, and three bedrooms on the

Hill Camp with its newly built icehouse.

PHOTO: LOUIS W. HILL SR., 1901 – MINNESOTA HISTORICAL SOCIETY

first floor. A screened porch spanned three sides and the entire front of the house. The house had a pitched roof and was constructed almost entirely of spruce logs. The bark was retained on the outside of the walls, and the inside walls were hewed off and wainscotting attached. Remarkably, all the wood was clear and without knots. The logs were long and straight with very little taper. The black spruce logs from the area were well known for their tight rings and tall straight structure. No wonder the house looked so good when it was finished! The total construction cost was $12,207.16.

Persistence was the key to success, and Hill's employees had been very persistent. When James J. Hill stepped off the launch and into his canoe to embark on his second trip to the St. John River, everything was ready. Hill wired his wife Mary on June 18, 1901: "Arrived yesterday. Party all well. Everything pleasant." Indeed it was! According to John Toomey, in a letter to his brother on June 20:

I was the last of the party to reach the house and Mr. Hill had finished his first inspection and the others had nearly gotten over their expressions of surprise and delight at the appearance of things when I arrived, but still there was enough said in my hearing to make me feel proud. The house is a thing of beauty …I had expected something fine, but it is larger and finer than I had imagined. It is to be regretted that we have no photographer in the party. I have reason to think that Mr. Hill is well pleased.

After the fishing party left the river in 1901, the houses were closed for the season and canoes were taken to the village for repairs. Then, preparations began, both on the river and in the railway office in St. Paul, for the 1902 season.

James J. Hill's three close friends arrive to inspect the new house, shortly after its completion in 1901. They would accompany Hill on many fishing trips in the future. *Left to right:* Colonel Daniel Lamont, Samuel Thorne, and George Baker.

Above: An old property blaze mark on a silver birch tree above Hill Camp's main house. One of the most common methods used to mark a property line was to disfigure a tree with an axe cut that would remain visible on the tree for many years. Another way to mark the property line at the time was to bury broken pottery at strategic points along its perimeter.

PHOTO: MARI HILL HARPUR, 2008 – PERSONAL COLLECTION

Facing: Eight guides standing on the shore below the camp with their paddles and poles ready to embark in the canoes. William Boyle is the head guide. He is holding a pole and is the tallest man in the middle with the white hat. He came from Grande-Rivière on the Gaspé peninsula. Other members of the Boyle family would continue to serve Hill Camp.
Left to right: Joseph Paquet, Sonny Chambers, Ben Chambers, William Boyle, James Chambers, two unidentified men, John Chambers, unidentified Gaspé man.

PHOTO: LOUIS W. HILL SR., 1910 – MHH PERSONAL COLLECTION

William Boyle, from Gaspé, served Hill as head guide for several years. Daniel Davies also hired him to research the river in 1898, when James J. Hill was searching for a river.

PHOTO: LOUIS W. HILL SR., 1910 – MHH PERSONAL COLLECTION

Fishermen Arriving and Surviving (1900 – 1916)

"Lots of salmon going up the River as the boys saw them all along the River on their way up [to] clean up the houses."

–Benjamin Chambers in a letter to James J. Hill, June 16, 1900

On his first trip to the St. John River in 1900, Hill's party consisted of his sons—Louis Sr. and Walter—and friends George Baker, Colonel Daniel Lamont (vice-president of Northern Pacific Railway), and Dr. Charles Smith (Hill's St. Paul physician). Of this group, Louis Sr., Baker, and Lamont would make many future trips to the camp with Hill. The party fished the river from July 2 to July 11 and took a total of 236 salmon, totalling 1,408 kg (3,104 lbs). Hill brought five hundred cigars with him from the Minnesota Club in St. Paul. Celebrations were the order of the day.

Going to the fishing camp was a complicated process because it was so remote. One thing that eased the travel for Hill and his guests was that in 1900 he purchased a steam yacht, *Eleanor*, which he renamed *Wacouta*, a Sioux word meaning "red wing." On several occasions Hill and members of his party boarded the yacht in

The *Wacouta*

Wacouta, an 804-ton yacht, was built at Bath, Maine, in 1894. She was originally named Eleanor. *She was leased by the Navy in April 1917.*

—Department of the Navy, Naval Historical Center

In 1900 James J. Hill purchased a steam yacht, *Eleanor*, which he renamed *Wacouta*. The yacht measured 240 feet and carried a crew of thirty-five to forty-five men. It was a true luxury vessel, with ten staterooms, four of which were part of a family suite on the main deck that also included two bathrooms. The yacht had six other bathrooms and eight water closets. There were four small cabins for servants in the aft section. The oak-panelled dining room and salon had fireplaces of

Venetian tile, Tiffany lamps, oriental rugs, and oak parquet floors. There was a large social hall, and an elegant stairway connected the main deck to the salon and guest rooms below. The yacht was equipped with electric lights and fans, a steam laundry with rotary washing machines and a drying room, a five-foot-deep refrigerator that ran the full width of the vessel, and an ice-making machine that helped preserve the salmon killed on the St. John River. The *Wacouta* was berthed in New London, Connecticut, under the stewardship of Captain David Weed. As captain, Weed was in charge of his ship and looked after every detail. During the fishing season,

he would purchase staples and cleaning supplies in New York and sail to Montreal or Quebec to take on perishables. He would then pick up his passengers for their trip to the St. John River. Captain Weed worked on the *Wacouta* for the entire period Hill owned her.

Above: Good friends on their way to Hill Camp.
Left to right: Captain David Weed, George Stewart,
Charles Steele, and Samuel Thorne on the deck of the
Wacouta.

PHOTO: LOUIS W. HILL SR. – MINNESOTA HISTORICAL SOCIETY

Facing page, sidebar, top: In 1900 James J. Hill purchased
a steam yacht, *Eleanor,* that he renamed *Wacouta.*

PHOTOGRAPHER UNKNOWN – MINNESOTA HISTORICAL SOCIETY

Sidebar, bottom: Arriving at St. John in lifeboats from
the *Wacouta.*

MHH PERSONAL COLLECTION

Facing: Side view of the *Wacouta* with a frigate
docked alongside, a man moving between the vessels.
Manoeuvring from the ship to the frigate was a
dangerous business. In rough waters, the fishing party
would have to wait for calm seas before disembarking.

PHOTO: LOUIS W. HILL SR. – MINNESOTA HISTORICAL SOCIETY

New York City for the trip to the river. Often, however, the fishing party went by train to Quebec City, where they boarded the *Wacouta* on the St. Lawrence River.

On June 27, 1900, the *Wacouta* left New York to arrive in Quebec City, where her crew loaded canoes and additional supplies before the fishing party boarded. The party arrived at the river on July 2, having travelled two days by water. Once at the river, Captain Weed had to navigate the river's mouth, particularly the sandbar, at high tide. The crew needed to offload the frigates and sail on to what is today known as Frigate Pool. There the canoes that had been launched from the village met the fishing party, and the canoe men poled up the river. According to Toomey, "When fishing is done from boats each rod requires one canoe and two boatmen." Payroll records show nineteen canoe men attended that first group.

During the fishing trip, the crew of the *Wacouta* who had remained on board, froze, packaged, and shipped the fresh salmon to family members, friends and business associates, politicians, and charitable institutions. The salmon would arrive with a card reading, "We are shipping you today one [or more] salmon which Mr. Hill would like you to accept with his compliments. It is of the number killed by Mr. Hill and his party on River St. John, Mingan, Quebec, recently. Trusting it will arrive in due course and in good condition."

James J. Hill arrived on June 17, 1901, for his second fishing trip. This was a special trip for Hill, not only because the house was completed but also because one of his guests was Grover Cleveland, former president of the United States (1885 – 1889 and 1893 – 1897). James J. Hill had accompanied Cleveland on his yacht, the *Susquehanna,* on numerous

Above: James J. Hill's great friend, Colonel Daniel Lamont, in a canoe with the guide holding his recent catch. This photo is not dated; however, in 1904 Lamont records his largest salmon at 14.6 kg (31 lbs).

Photo: Louis W. Hill Sr. – Minnesota Historical Society

Left: A canoe filled with one day's salmon catch. The fish are ready to be sent to the *Wacouta* to be processed and packed in ice for shipment to many of James J. Hill's friends.

Photo: Louis W. Hill Sr. – Minnesota Historical Society

Opposite page: One of the numerous books that contained all the fishing records of the Hill Camp catch over the years.

St. John River Records, 1912 – Minnesota Historical Society

Below: A mailing label used for shipping salmon to Hill's many friends and business associates.

St. John River Ephemera – Minnesota Historical Society

ONE SALMON

To

Compliments of Mr. James J. Hill

fishing trips on the Atlantic during his presidencies. Mary Hill wrote in her diary on July 28, 1888: "We hear Papa is fishing with President Cleveland and party." *The New York Times* reported on the 1888 trip: "President Cleveland and a party of five, consisting of Postmaster-General Dickinson, Col. Daniel Lamont, Joseph Stickney of New York, Smith M. Weed of Plattsburg, and James J. Hill of Minneapolis, Minnesota are chumming for bluefish at Fire Island today."

Cleveland fished for six days at James J. Hill's camp and took twelve salmon. He did not visit the river again; however, his private

secretary and Secretary of War (1893–1897), Colonel Daniel Lamont, accompanied him on that 1901 trip and did return every summer until his death, shortly after returning from Hill Camp on July 23, 1905.

Perhaps because of the age of many of the men who came to the river and its remote location, a physician was always a member of the fishing party. Dr. George Stewart was George Baker's personal physician and also attended to the medical needs of the Hill family while they were in New York City. Dr. Stewart, head of the Department of Surgery at New York's Bellevue Hospital, was

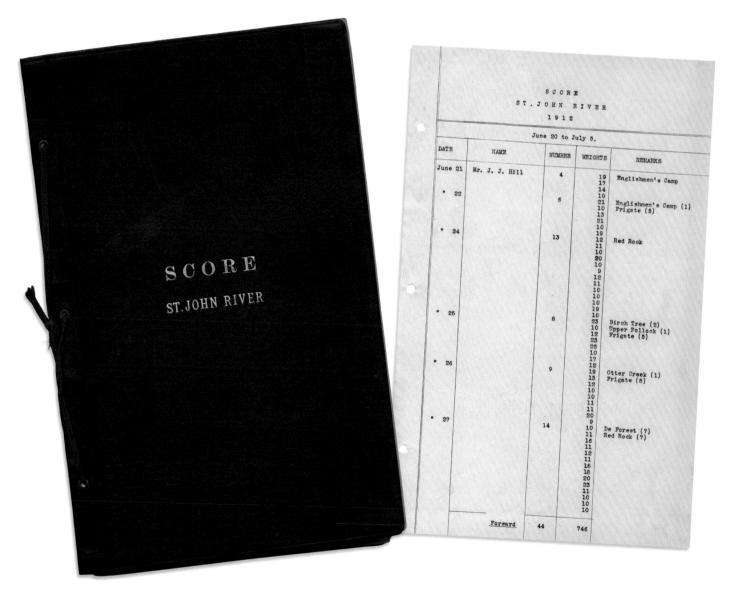

the physician who first made the trip in 1902, and he continued to join the fishing party for the majority of the following years that Hill fished the river. Dr. Stewart's nickname on the trips was "Big Medicine," and he was an important contributor to the evening entertainment, which often consisted of Scottish songs, poems, and tales. On June 27 of the 1906 trip, Samuel Thorne set the record for number of salmon killed in one day when he returned to camp with twenty salmon. The resident poet, unnamed but presumably Dr. Stewart, celebrated Thorne's feat in verse:

Thorne's record was only broken twice during Hill's time at the river. In 1908 Hill took twenty-one salmon, and the next year Louis Sr. equalled his father's catch.

The year 1909 must have been an especially jolly time on the river, as Hill had arranged for professional entertainment for the fishing trip. On June 4, 1909, Toomey wrote W.T. Hetherington, Great Northern Railway's agent in the company's Montreal office:

To Uncle Sam Thorne

A dusty Miller –
The waters cool
That gracefully ripples
The Frigate Pool.

A dusty Miller –
The sunshine bright,
And he sailed that Frigate
From morn till night.

A dusty Miller –
A goodly man,
And he wielded that killer
As none other can.

A dusty Miller –
Twenty fish risen.
And killed before sunset.
And the Record's his'n.

Dr. George "Big Medicine" Stewart by the fireplace at the Deforest camp.
PHOTO: LOUIS W. HILL SR., 1905 – MINNESOTA HISTORICAL SOCIETY

We will want a Scotch piper to accompany Mr. Hill and party on the fishing trip this year to the lower St. Lawrence in the yacht Wacouta, *and would like your assistance in looking up and selecting a suitable man to fill the place. We can guarantee three weeks engagement and would like to have it understood that the piper would remain as long as he might be wanted. We would expect the piper to, of course, have everything complete in the way of costume, regalia, etc. and above all to be an A-1 performer on the pipes, and to also have an appearance in keeping with his calling.*

Hetherington replied on June 9: "Would advise that I have located a man that I can thoroughly recommend …in the person of Pipe-Major D. Manson of the 5th Royal Highlanders of this City. Pipe-Major Manson is the champion of the Dominion and is Piper to the St. James Club of this City and has everything needed in the way of regalia, costume, etc." The services of Mr. Manson were engaged at the rate of $25.00 per week with "board and sleeping accommodation."

Over the years Hill's guest list did not vary greatly. It seemed important to him to have among his fellow fishermen family and close friends, whom he had known for many years in New York and Minnesota. These friends were from the elite of the eastern investment and banking establishment and also railroad executives: Geof Baker, founder of the First National Bank of New York; Samuel Thorne, banker and president of the Pennsylvania Coal Co.; George Clark, investment banker with Clark, Dodge & Co.; Daniel Scott Lamont, Chief of Staff to President Cleveland, and former Secretary of War; Charles Steele and Henry P. Davison, both partners with J.P. Morgan & Co.; and Jule Hannaford, Charles Bunn, William Dean, Judge William Hook, and William Dunwoody, Minnesota friends and business associates.

The "regulars" at the river always looked forward to the trips. Charles Steele wired Hill on June 6, 1912: "Have you any idea when you will start for the Promised Land?" Steele, who would join Hill at the river for seven years, made an unusual deduction after the 1909 trip. That year the total weight of the fish killed was 4,605 kg (10,153 lbs), making it the second largest quantity to be caught in a single season on the river. Perhaps the kill weight

that year was affected by what Steele observed when he wrote to Hill on July 28, 1909: "You will be quite interested, as a matter of natural history, to learn that in one of the fish which were killed in the St. Johns [sic] this year several good sized stones were found, some of them half the size of a man's fist. Perhaps if you see Mr. Sam Thorne it would interest him to know about this and he might make a note of it in his little red book."

Charles Steele writes a newsy letter on July 26, 1909, about the river stones found in a salmon's stomach and its recorded weight.

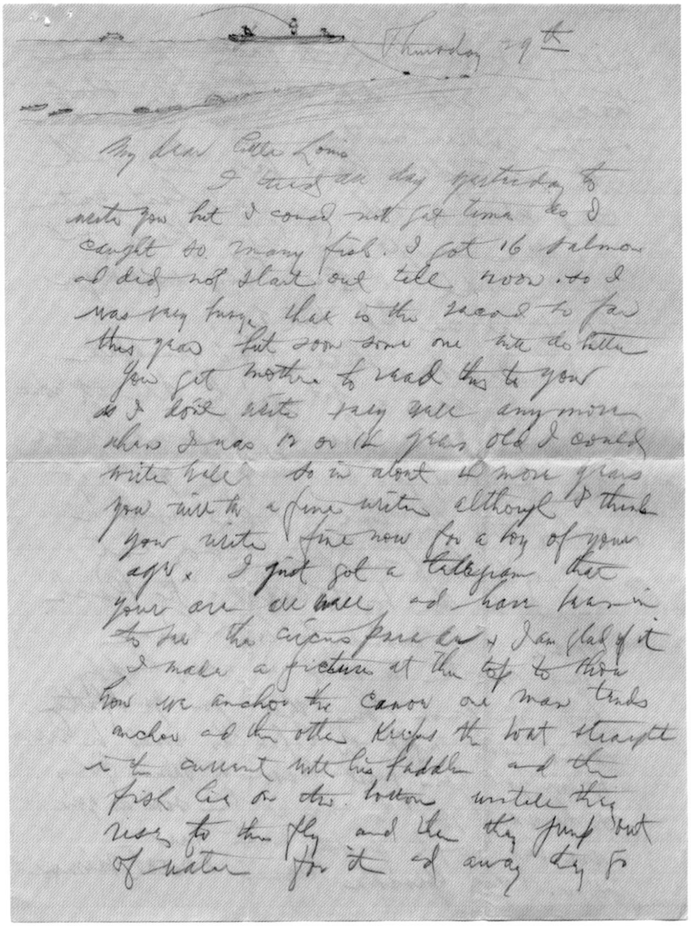

Pages one and three of a letter written by Louis Hill Sr. on June 29, 1911, complete with pencil drawings. Page three describes one of the drawings: "This picture shows how you come to shore with the fish and the man watches with a net until he can land him for you."

MHH PERSONAL COLLECTION

Family members would also enliven the fishing party. James J. Hill's third child, Louis Sr., was a constant companion to his father. He was devoted to family as well as to the outdoors. In 1904 Louis Sr. had the distinction of taking the largest salmon ever properly recorded on the river, weighing 16.6 kg (36.5 lbs). A carved wooden image of that salmon hangs today on the wall of the log house at the Hill Camp (see the frontispiece). Louis Hill Sr. fished with his father eleven times and brought his son Louis Jr. for three visits, in 1912, 1914, and 1915.

In 1911, the year before his son joined him on the river, Louis Sr. wrote to Louis Jr. from the camp, describing how one fishes for salmon. In the letter, Louis Sr. includes pencil drawings of three men in canoe: "I made a picture at the top to show how we anchor the canoe, one man tends anchor and the other keeps the boat straight in the current with his paddle and the fish lie on the bottom until they rise to the fly and then they jump out of the water for it and away they go."

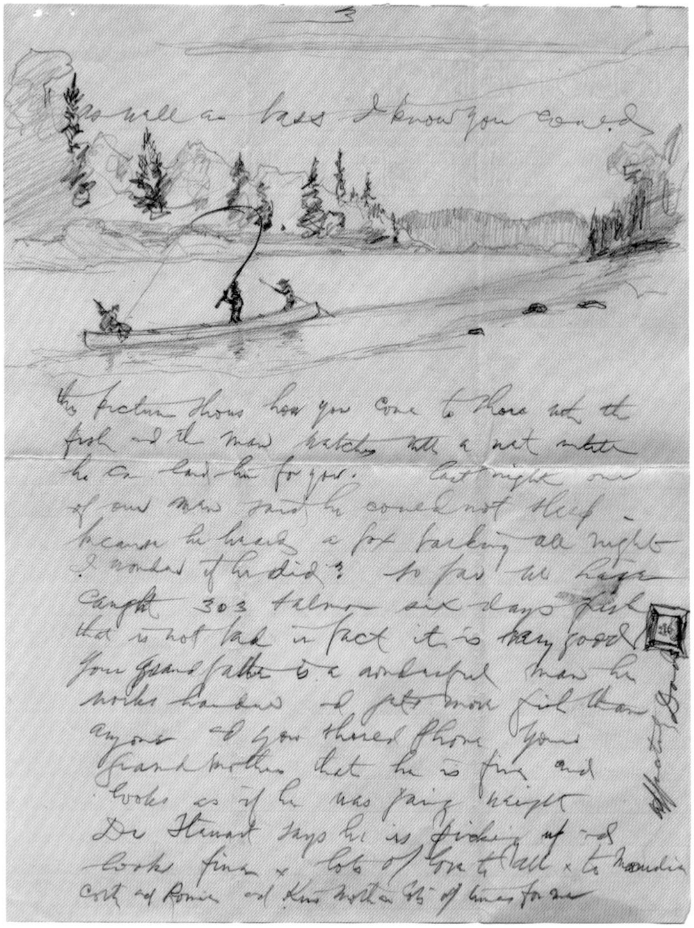

During the fishing trip of 1913, Louis Sr. wrote to his son about his latest experience. The yacht had arrived at the mouth of the river on June 22 and was still waiting the following day, "for the bar to become quiet enough to cross." Louis's letter goes on to tell of visiting Mingan, the next village east from St-Jean. There the

fishermen met a Mr. Scott, a retired employee of the Hudson's Bay Company, and Louis invited back to the yacht for dinner. Scott told stories of the early days of the area, the wildlife, and his method for "starting a salmon" by pinning a paper funnel to the line and letting the current carry it down to the fish, "so it would cover his eyes like a blind-fold, the fish runs wild and sometimes will run up on the bank …This is something new and Dr. Stewart and I are going to try it."

Typically, life at the camp took on the rhythm of a small village as the seasons came and went. New and old friends and family made the annual trip to the St. John River. Sunday services were held on the porch, and visits to town were rare. A strong sense of companionship and friendly competition prevailed, as is shown in the careful recording of kills in the Salmon Record book. Catch was recorded and tackle discussed at length. When the salmon returned to the river to spawn, the sports were ready to welcome

Above: A group of guides with their catch. Bob Minor, third from the right, holds the "big fish."
PHOTO: LOUIS W. HILL SR. – MINNESOTA HISTORICAL SOCIETY

Right: This is believed to be Louis W. Hill Sr.'s 1906 record fish, which had the distinction of being the largest salmon ever properly recorded on the St. John River, at 16.5 kg (36.5 lbs). It is held here by Robert (Bob) Minor, James J. Hill's steward.
PHOTO: LOUIS W. HILL SR. – MINNESOTA HISTORICAL SOCIETY

them back, and all the preparations for the day's fishing were readied. A regular routine was followed to ensure that everything would be set for Hill and his guests. Once the guests had left, Robert Chambers carefully matched Toomey's inventory list with what was actually at the camp and reported on any discrepancies. Canoes were repaired and buildings winterized. It was always a busy place, any time of the year, and there was plenty to do.

This series of images shows a fishing party getting into canoes at Hill Camp, moving down the river, and arriving at the village of St-Jean. These photographs were taken during the party's final departure. They would not return until the following year.

Chapter Four

A Daily Rhythm

(1912 – 1916)

"Amis makousham: indigenous annual meeting time, where friends unite."

—William Ashley Anderson, *Angel of Hudson Bay* (translated from Innu by Maud Watts)

Louis W. Hill Jr. with feathered friends: two red-tail hawk fledglings.

PHOTO: LOUIS W. HILL SR., 1910 – MHH PERSONAL COLLECTION

Louis W. Hill Jr. holding a large fish by the side of the river with two guides.

PHOTO: LOUIS W. HILL SR., 1910 – MHH PERSONAL COLLECTION

Settlements like the village of St-Jean commonly have great community spirit. The remoteness of the location, the inclement weather, and the scarcity of food make working together an essential feature of everyday existence. Everyone in the community takes part in surviving, no matter how difficult the circumstances, and everyone also enjoys those moments when they can join together in friendship. That same quality of companionship and community spirit would come to permeate Hill Camp.

When the summer of 1912 had arrived, it was time, again, for all the friends to gather together, and John Toomey was, as usual, at the camp early, making sure everything was in order.

Louis Jr. with three guides preparing a shore lunch at the lower pools. For many years it was common for the sports who fished the lower part of the river to eat their lunch streamside on account of the time it took to pole upriver. Those who were fishing closer to camp would return to the house to eat. *Left to right:* Robert (Sonny) Chambers, unknown guide, John Chambers, Louis W. Hill Jr.

PHOTO: LOUIS W. HILL SR. – MINNESOTA HISTORICAL SOCIETY

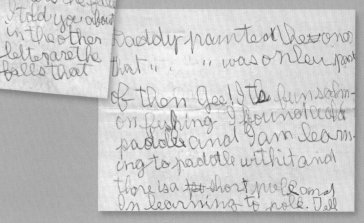

The two-page letter Louis Jr. sent to his mother on July 8, 1912. "Dear Mother R.M.C. [Romie, Maudie, Corty (siblings)], Cub and others—the falls I told you about in the other letter are the falls where the Indians have a bear in a trap and we saw them going up to shoot it. Love, Louis."

MHH PERSONAL COLLECTION

Louis Jr. stands in the canoe with his guide, Sonny Chambers, who is holding a fish. Notice the handmade hood that sports wore to protect themselves from the hateful black flies that are so abundant in the early part of the fishing season.

MINNESOTA HISTORICAL SOCIETY

Ten-year-old Louis Jr., looking through a collection of eleven fish.

PHOTO: LOUIS W. HILL – MINNESOTA HISTORICAL SOCIETY

James J. Hill battles a salmon at the side of the river.
PHOTO: LOUIS W. HILL SR. – MHH PERSONAL COLLECTION

James J. Hill admires the same fish, his recent catch.
PHOTO: LOUIS W. HILL SR. – MINNESOTA HISTORICAL SOCIETY

Toomey sailed from the camp to meet the group in Montreal as they arrived on the *Wacouta*. Meanwhile, Louis Sr., Louis Jr., William Hood Dunwoody, and James Hill's steward, Bob Minor (who helped prepare the sports for their daily routine and also cooked at the camp), arrived in Montreal aboard Hill's private railway car from St. Paul, Minnesota. Hill, Charles Steele, and Dr. Stewart came by rail from New York City. On June 18 all were assembled and boarded the yacht for the trip to the mouth of the river. They arrived at the "Promised Land" on June 19. Once there, they were ready to indulge. They fully immersed themselves in the sport of fishing, honouring a selection of feather flies, and extolling the technique of the fly rod.

It was another festive event. Hill's son and eldest grandson, the two Louis W. Hills, had each celebrated a birthday on May 19, just over a month before. The elder man was forty, and the younger ten years old. Dunwoody, an old friend of Hill's and a Minneapolis milling executive, was as anxious as any of them to start the festivities. All were looking forward to the trip. Fortunately, the fishing party recorded their personal observations, and their letters to relatives and friends reveal an intimate portrait of this particular fishing season at the camp.

Mr. Dunwoody with guide and fish in canoe, 1912.
PHOTO: LOUIS W. HILL SR., 1912 – MINNESOTA HISTORICAL SOCIETY

Louis Sr. distributing candy and cookies to the village children.
PHOTO: UNKNOWN – MINNESOTA HISTORICAL SOCIETY

That year, the group took 753 salmon, with a total weight of 4,696.5 kg (10,354 lb), beating the previous record for total fish taken, set in 1909. Dr. Stewart was high-man, at 132, with three others taking over one hundred salmon each. Louis Jr., on his inaugural trip, took fifty salmon, one weighing 14 kg (31 lb). What an experience for the young lad! Louis Sr. wired St. Paul often to let those at home know what his son had accomplished. On June 24 he reported, "Louis is fishing very well. Has killed seventeen. Got six today. He does as well as some of the men. All well, send love."

Samuel Thorne had been ill and was not expected to make the trip; however, on June 21 he wired Hill that he had recovered and he and his son, Edwin, would join the others if the *Wacouta* could pick them up at Rimouski on June 24. The fishing party was now in full swing. Thorne's trip was beneficial to his health, as was noted in a letter Edwin wrote: "One great source of added pleasure to me, as I know it was to you, was to see Father's daily improvement and he certainly appeared different when he left us at Poughkeepsie from what he did when we returned there on our outward journey."

Dunwoody also wrote of improved health after the fishing trip: "We reached home in due time and I am greeted by all with, 'how fine you look and you have gained weight', and I indeed do feel that I have been greatly benefitted by the trip."

Louis Sr. did not ignore the residents and their children who lived in the village of St-Jean. A letter from Toomey to Captain Weed contains the following instructions:

> Please note when you reach Montreal to purchase four pails of common, mixed candies and about a barrel full of cookies and gingersnaps, and have the candies and cookies put up separately in half-pound or one-pound bags. Mr. L. W. Hill's attention should be brought to the matter of these candies and cookies when you reach St. John River, so that he will give directions as to the distribution to be made of them.

Dunwoody acknowledged in a letter to his brother, Evan, on May 6, 1912, that he "had never tried salmon fishing." Whether it was beginner's luck or natural fishing skill, Dunwoody took eighty-four salmon on the 1912 trip. Perhaps it was the relaxed atmosphere at camp that encouraged Dunwoody's latent skills, as Dunwoody further wrote on July 10, 1913:

> Our dinner was ready for us at ten o'clock always and we usually took an hour to eat dinner, and then sat up until midnight relating our experiences, while Mr. Hill put in

Dunwoody's photograph of Louis Jr. with "three hands." The guide on the right is Benjamin Chambers Sr.

Fishing Fashion Riverside

Top to bottom: James J. Hill in a hood made by his wife, Mary; dressed in Sunday whites; and in fishing attire.

WILLIAM H. DUNWOODY.
MINNEAPOLIS, MINN.

July 23rd, 1912.

Dear Louis:—
                I wondered while we were out
on the trip, why it was that you were so
good at fishing, paddling and poling. I
know now, as my camera has found you out.
I enclose you one of the pictures. You
did not tell me that you had three hands.
You must have had one of them up your
sleeve. Perhaps you have heard about the
man that was always carrying something up
his sleeve to bring out on important occasions; and you have been carrying yours
all the time without letting us know anything about it.
                I hope you found mother and the
brothers and sister all right, when you
got to Seattle. I know that they were
glad to see you and I am sure they must
have said that you look fine and that
your muscles have grown stronger.
                This was a fine outing for all of us.
I gained in weight(as I am sure you and
the others did) three pounds now more than
I ever weighed.
                I hope you are having a good time.
                Yours truly,

                Wm. H. Dunwoody

After the 1912 trip was over, Dunwoody sent a note to Louis Jr. on July 23, 1912, with the photograph on the facing page enclosed.

most of his time making puzzle pictures from the sawed blocks which you often see. He gave himself up wholly to the pleasures of the outing and to the fishing; said nothing about business or politics. Some papers came to the house in the same mail with your letter, but he did not look at them; did not seem to be interested in anything aside from what he was doing. He works well in looking after business and when it is done, it is usually well done and he can give his entire thought to something else.

Dunwoody continued to describe the fishing schedule in another letter to his brother Evan on July 10, 1913:

We did have a fine time; fishing not quite so good as it was last year; the water was low and very clear and the fish could see our boat and were afraid of us. It is so far North that the weather is quite cool there generally. Although the party was small we had twenty men who went up the River with us, boatmen, cooks, etc., and there were forty men on the yacht, which lay anchored at the mouth of the St. John; so that altogether it required sixty men to take care of us five in this River experience. Mr. Hill is an ideal host, doing everything

These long Spey rods, named after the famous Scottish fishing river, had to be cast with both hands.

PHOTO: LOUIS W. HILL SR. – MINNESOTA HISTORICAL SOCIETY

One day's catch.

PHOTO: LOUIS W. HILL SR. – MINNESOTA HISTORICAL SOCIETY

Samuel Thorne landing a salmon.

PHOTO: LOUIS W. HILL SR. – MINNESOTA HISTORICAL SOCIETY

Returning to camp after an evening fish. This must have
been the last cast, and there is a fish at the end of the
bent rod. The guides are holding the canoe in the current
using their poles.

PHOTO: LOUIS W. HILL SR. – MINNESOTA HISTORICAL SOCIETY

*that is possible for his guests. He came to my room several
times to know whether there was anything that he could do
for me; he did furnish me with salmon flies, a fine pig-skin
book for the salmon flies, and a waterproof sack to put all
my things in when in the boat, and Louie furnished me
with a nice brown Scotch sweater and fishing hat, as well as
green glasses to be used when the Sun shone brightly. Mr.
Hill was very bright and cheerful, many mornings he would
walk the porch for half an hour singing songs and hymns.*

Dunwoody goes on to tell a "fish tale" about his hooking a salmon in the tail and landing the fish: "Mr. Hill says this is a fish story that few would believe and I am ready to assent to this."

Many of the men who accompanied Hill to fish the St. John River were getting older, including Hill himself. They appreciated more and more the rest and company of close friends, as much as the fine sport of the annual trip. Hill would have three more summer trips to the river; however, Dunwoody would only make one more visit there, in 1913.

When young Louis was unable to make the fishing trip the following year, his father wrote him that everyone on the trip was disappointed at his absence:

*Mr. Dunwoody missed you very much when he got on the
car Wednesday night, leaving St. Paul, and when we arrived
at Montreal your Grandfather was disappointed as he had
hoped and expected you would come along, and so was Dr.
Stewart and Mr. Steel [Steele] disappointed, as they were
looking for you. It is nice to know your Grandfather's friends
are so fond of you.*

*We went into Gaspé Sunday morning at daylight and picked
up ten canoe-men and two dozen lobsters. The canoe-men
were all looking for you and your man was particularly
disappointed that you had not come.*

In 1913 and 1914, Samuel Thorne, who was perhaps Hill's closest friend, also could not make the trip to the St. John River as he was recovering from a heart attack. Thorne was able to return to the river in 1915 and fished every day from June 26 to July 3, coming back to camp with a 12.7 kg (28 lbs) salmon on that last day. The next morning, Thorne had a fatal heart attack. His son, William, had accompanied him to the river, and he and Louis Sr. made all the arrangements to break camp immediately and return his body to New York.

Hill took the deaths of his old friends very hard. As more of his friends and business associates passed away, he must have felt his own time shortening. Hill's own health problems, related to complications from hemorrhoid symptoms, were beginning to surface in ways that restricted his activities. Sadly, he died in his St. Paul home on May 29, 1916, just a few days short of when he would have ordinarily started for camp.

In former years, this was about the time Sonny Chambers would also be sending letters and telegrams to Hill, reporting on the conditions on the river. However, Sonny himself had died the previous fall, in 1915, and his wife, Esther Wright, had taken over as guardian of the river. On June 13, 1916, her son, Robert Chambers Jr., wrote Toomey:

*A few lines to let you know condition of the River. Getting
a few salmon in the nets outside the River. We began to see
the salmon in the lower part of the River. Will let you know
when the salmon are in the pools. Everything in good order.
Please let me know before party come and how many men
will be wanted. I am very sorry to learn of the death of Mr.
Hill my good father. I do not know how I will get along for
he was so good to us all. I remain your obedient servant.*

The era of James J. Hill and Benjamin and Sonny Chambers had come to a close. However, the story of the St. John River and its connection to both the Hill and Chambers families continued. Life on the river resumed for a new generation of these families, as well as the ever-returning salmon.

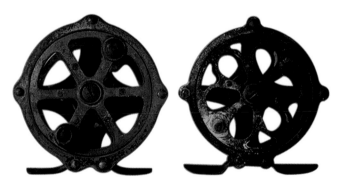

Two reels made by Sunnybrook Union Hardware Co., Torrington, Conn., USA.
Photo: Mari Hill Harpur, 2013 – From the Private Collection of the River Wye

James J. Hill, Lord Grey and an unidentified member of Lord
Grey's fishing party, in front of Hill Camp, probably in 1911.

Chapter Five

Traditions and Transitions: Women and Men Fishing (1901 – 1987)

"The Great Sea has sent me adrift,

It moves me as a weed in a great river,

Earth and the Great Weather move me,

Have carried me away

And move my inward parts with joy."

– Uvanuk, a woman shaman of the Igloolik,
quoted by Knud Rasmussen

Numerous individuals have found creative inspiration when visiting Hill Camp, and Ann Mitchell was one of them. She and her husband, Brad, spent several seasons as guests. In order to create this painting, Ann drew on her experiences of Hill Camp life during the 1980s and the stories that were told to her. Various members of the Hill family are depicted, among them James J. Hill III, who at the time operated a fire-prevention equipment company. He can be seen running with a hose to pour water on the cooking fire at the beach. Anselme (Sam) Beaudin is shown talking to Doug Harpur while he points to an airplane in the sky. Sam, who had rarely left the local area, had just questioned Doug about how many people travelled in the passenger planes which flew daily over the camp toward Europe. Doug had answered, "Oh, about 350 people." Sam's eyes grew very large, and his reply was, "*Imagine, deux villages!*" Below the icehouse on the beach stands a gentleman with two fish in his hands: Colonel Ken Dyer, whose presence at camp made the fish nervous. Ken always caught two fish on the first day he arrived. Mari is weighing a fish at the scale by the steps. She wears pearls in hopes that they will bring her luck. A moose family crosses the river above the camp, while a black bear stands by the marking stones waiting for someone to give it a fish.

Painting: Ann Mitchell, 1997 – MHH Personal Collection

A Woman's River Too

John Brown once referred to the St. John River as "an old man's river." He could have just as easily described it as "a woman's river," for many women have enjoyed and fished its waters. Typically during that period, women were not always accounted for in the records. However, it is through their affection for the sport and their substantial narratives, found in their letters and diaries, that we see another aspect to camp life. Several women—Lady Sybil Grey, daughter of Lord Grey, the Governor General of Canada (1904 – 1911), Hill's wife Mary and granddaughter, Georgiana Slade (1912), and Elsi Hill and Meredith Alden (1970s and 1980s), and many others—left wonderful accounts of the activities in which they took part at Hill Camp. Their collective experiences speak to

the transition from the early years of the twentieth century to the present. This river welcomed all: the observers and the novices and the professional women and men who held the sport of salmon fishing close to their hearts.

In 1901 Hill Camp had hosted its first honeymooning couple. James J. Hill's son, Louis, brought his new wife, Maud Van Cortlandt Taylor Hill, to camp after their wedding in New York City at the beginning of June. Louis and Maud sailed to the St. John on the *Wacouta* for a few days of fishing, even though it was early in the year. The couple met up with the incoming Hill party in Quebec City. Toomey wired the St. Paul office: "L. W. H. and his bride left the yacht shortly after our getting on board. I saw the former for a few minutes only but did not see the latter. Maud caught a twelve-

pound salmon …and observed with enthusiasm that it was 'great sport'."

In 1907 Lord and Lady Grey and their daughters Lady Sybil and Lady Evelyn, as well as Mr. Arthur Sladen, Lord Grey's aide, arrived on July 5. They had been fishing on the nearby Mingan River. Lady Grey and Lady Evelyn remained at Hill's camp for only one day while Lord Grey and Lady Sybil remained there until July 15, three days after Hill's party had left the river. The letters Lady Sybil Grey sent to Hill are primarily descriptive narratives of the sport. She and her mother and sister were among that small number of elite women guests who fished the St. John River during Hill's time.

The Greys' catch was comparable to all others on the St. John River. Lady Sybil Grey took a 13.6 kg (30 lb) salmon. A letter Lady Sybil sent to Hill on July 15, 1907 not only thanked him for his hospitality but also carefully reported the fishing results, including pools fished and flies used, for the days after he left the river. Lady Sybil also included the following blow-by-blow account of her struggle to land an elusive salmon::

> *Alas! We have just left your magnificent river. No words can say what pleasant recollections we take away with us of the good times you gave us. I have never enjoyed a 10 days more and I shall always remember it, & your great kindness to us with gratitude and pleasure. I am enclosing a list of the fish and where we caught them. We arrived at Mingan on Tuesday morning & found that Evy [sister, Lady Evelyn Grey] & Mother had killed quite a number of fish. The river is swarming with them, but is terribly high. Yesterday Mother killed 10 fish! Evy 8, myself 6 & father 5.*

The total number of salmon taken by both groups in 1907 was 342, totaling 2,330 kg (5,137 lb). Hill's total was forty-one salmon, taken in twelve days of fishing. The top prize went to Lord Grey, who took fifty-seven salmon in seven days. Lady Sybil, fishing the same number of days, came in a close second with fifty-four salmon taken, and her 13.6 kg (30 lb) salmon was the largest taken that season.

The Grey party returned in 1908, arriving on July 2, the day after Hill's party left. Hill himself remained for the entirety of Grey's visit, fishing for eighteen days that year. Lord and Lady Grey sent James J. Hill a Christmas card that year (following page), accompanied by a calendar and a letter from Sybil, as well as a photograph of her at Hill Camp.

The Grey party in front of Hill Camp in 1908 (left to right): Lord Grey, possibly Charles Steele, James J. Hill, Lady Sybil Grey, and likely Mr. Frewen and Captain Pickering.

PHOTO: LOUIS W. HILL SR. – MINNESOTA HISTORICAL SOCIETY

Opposite page: Lady Grey dries her fly line while Lord Grey stands nearby on the front porch at Hill Camp. At that time, the lines were made of silk, and conscientious sports would need to air dry them by removing them from the reel every evening. Lord Grey was the fourth Earl Grey who served as Governor General and Commander-in-Chief of the Dominion of Canada (1904 – 1911). The Governor General was a great friend of Hill's. Lady Grey visited the camp twice, in 1907 and 1911.

PHOTO: LOUIS W. HILL SR. – MHH PERSONAL COLLECTION

The postcard below was accompanied by a letter, dated December 25, 1908, on Government House letterhead:

Dear Mr. Hill,

I am sending you a little calendar to wish you a very happy Xmas & New Year.

As you will see I have been conceited enough to send a photograph of myself & Phil Boyle on that glorious never to be forgotten day—I suppose I shall never have such a day fishing again—Fourteen fish the heaviest 30 lbs !!

Again with many wishes for the New Year.

Believe me,

Yours very sincerely,

Sybil Grey

The Christmas card sent to James J. Hill from Lord and Lady Grey, 1908. The photograph features Lady Sybil Grey and Phil Boyle with a string of fish. Below the photo are the words: "July 12, 14 fish. Weighing 218 lbs. Average 15 1/2 lbs."

Once again in 1910 Lord Grey made plans to visit Hill at the river. He was obligated to be in London but hoped to return in time to join Hill, or, if Hill's party had left, to use his camp. When Grey realized he would not be able to return in time to fish, he wrote Hill: "I am much disappointed to think that my enforced visit to England robs me of the pleasure to which I have been looking forward during the whole of the past year, to share with you the best sport in Canada."

Lady Sybil also wrote Hill of her disappointment, on June 8, 1910. "I must write you a line to tell you how brokenhearted I am that I shall not be a guest of yours on the St. John this year. I …was counting the days, almost the hours, until the happy moment came when father & I should start for the St. John—therefore the blow is bitter." She further wrote that she would rather fish than visit England, and that "some of the happiest moments of my life have been whilst staying …on the St. John."

When Hill sent the arrangements for their 1911 trip, Lord Grey wrote Hill on May 27, 1911: "Splendid—I wish you could have seen my daughter Sybil's jump of delight when I told her the contents of your letter. It was as good to see as the rise at one's fly of one of the biggest of your St. John salmon. I can be at the mouth of the St. John July 4 … looking forward much to a long Sunday talk with you and shall be greatly disappointed if I lose this." The plans held, and while the rest of Hill's party spent July 8 on the *Wacouta*, the two old friends went to the camp on Sunday to enjoy their "long Sunday talk."

The letters sent to Hill by Lord Grey and Lady Sybil shortly after the Greys left the camp on July 21 are long, full of praise for the sport, and contain many interesting details of their time with the salmon. Sybil's letter to Hill was written on July 21, from the yacht *Earl Grey* on its return to Montreal. The letter of was nine pages and went into details that only another fisher would understand and appreciate. She noted how much her mother enjoyed the sport: "I think she was the keenest of the lot, she simply loved it. She was always out first and in last."

James J. Hill is seated in a canoe. His daughter, Charlotte, can be seen in another canoe on the right edge of the photo. They are in Frigate Pool, preparing to pole up to the camp.

Both she and her father wrote of Sybil's encounter with the "whale":

> One day I went up and tried the [Island] Pool & a pool just below it round the corner—the men said it had no name so I named it "The Unlucky Pool." It was an extremely bright hot day & the fish were rising terribly short ...it really was disheartening. I couldn't get them to take hold properly—At last one took pin well & good. I thought he must be a big fish & then he jumped & to my terror & delight I saw that he was your whale Mr. Hill!! He jumped three times & really I think he was the biggest salmon I have ever seen. He was tremendously thick through & an immense length—my heart was in my mouth all the time. When I had him on about 10 minutes he went into the middle of the River & as Felix [Boyle, her guide] & I thought sank to the bottom & sulked there—We couldn't move him.

Sybil wrote of the fight going on for some time, of the attempts to net the salmon, and of the unhappy result: "[we] were just in the act of netting him when the hook came away, he slowly moved just out of reach & back into the deep water—After that we named the pool, 'The Unlucky Pool' & sadly headed our way homeward—that was my only sad day." Sybil's letter included a record of the fish taken by the party, which alas, did not include the "whale."

In 1912, after the fishing party left the river, Hill sailed to Montreal to meet his wife Mary. With their daughter, Charlotte Slade and family, they boarded the *Wacouta* and sailed back to the St. John River for their brief and only visit to the camp.

In her diary, Mary recorded her perspective of life on the river. The following excerpts include some insight on the difficulties that were often encountered by the fishermen arriving at the St. John River:

> July 6 – George, Charlotte, the children and I leave on the Soo [railway from St. Paul, Minnesota] this evening for Montreal to join Papa.
>
> July 8 – Arrived at Montreal on time. Papa, Mr. Thorne, Louis met us ...then went to Wacouta found Mr. Dunwoody and Louis Jr. there.

July 9 – Quebec (City). In the afternoon we all went in an auto to Montmorency (Falls) and St-Anne-de-Beaupreé went in to church... The auto George was in with the children had 4 blow outs then no more tires so all had to pack in to ours to get back.

July 10 – This morning we are all glad to come aboard the Wacouta. Coaling all over with.

July 12 – Arrived at Father Point yesterday, 7 p.m. Put off the Pilot then started for St. Johns River [Saguenay] Co[unty], arrived today at St. Johns River at 11 a.m. Started up the river in Launch but finished last hour and half in canoes arrived at Camp 4 p.m.

July 13 – At Camp on St. John's River Canada. A fine morning and how beautiful the River here is. The house too is most comfortable and nicely furnished ...7 bedrooms some large and 2 beds in them ...but the mosquitoes and flies! It is a beautiful spot. George, Charlotte and papa each killed a salmon, low water; warmer temperature has sent the salmon up the River.

July 14 – Rainy all day. We left the River St. John at 9 a.m., reached the mouth in canoes, 12 miles, at 11 a.m. As there had been a storm we could not cross the Bar so waited until 3 p.m. Even then it was rough but we got over and glad to reach Wacouta. Weather so bad we got inside Anticosti Island and lay still for the night. As we canoed down the river it rained part way. We made good time. Robert thoughtfully brought along some food and prepared lunch for us in R. Chambers' house. We all enjoyed the time at the fishing Camp house found it most comfortable ...Papa finished large puzzle. Captain Weed came over the Bar three times before he took us, it was rough very.

July 15 – At Gaspé Quebec Canada. We left the mouth of St. Johns River about 4 p.m. yesterday, went into rough seas and electric storm. Then we got inside of Anticosti Island. Stayed there until 10 p.m. Started out again then and had a very rough night until we reached Gaspé about 6 a.m.

Ann Mitchell displays her fish with guide Damas Beaudin and his nephew, Toussaint Beaudin, the *droppeur* in Frigate Pool.
PHOTO: MARI HILL HARPUR, 1997 – MHH PERSONAL COLLECTION

"My first salmon!" called out Nancy Jenkinson while I came to the side of the river to congratulate her and photograph the event. Donald Thom, her husband, holds the net while the guide, Anselme (Sam) Beaudin, keeps the canoe stable.
PHOTO: MARI HILL HARPUR, 1989 – MHH PERSONAL COLLECTION

The Hill family group sits on the side of Frigate Pool, waiting for the canoes. Mary Hill is seated with an umbrella, and Charlotte Hill Slade in a white shirt; Norman Slade is bent over holding the front of the canoe to the right of Georgiana, James J. Hill's granddaughter, the young girl in long braids running in the centre of the photo. The man bent over in the boat in a white hat could be James J. Hill, and George Slade is also part of the scene. There are four guides in attendance.
PHOTO: UNKNOWN – MINNESOTA HISTORICAL SOCIETY

While Mary's account of the 1912 visit to the river was written as it occurred, her granddaughter, Georgiana, wrote of the same visit some seventy years afterward. Here is how she remembered the trip she had taken as a nine-year-old:

> Grandpa had wanted to show Grandma the fishing camp in Canada where, for years, he and his friends had enjoyed their Salmon fishing vacations. In 1912, Father [George Slade] and Aunt Rachel [Rachel Hill, Hill's fifth daughter] had survived attacks of typhoid contracted at Jekyll Island, and father was recuperating at home. Grandpa thought it the ideal time for Grandma and the Slades to meet him in Montreal after his fishing party disbanded. They would board Grandpa's yacht, the Wacouta, and cruise from Montreal to New York via the St. John River. So, Grandma, Grandpa, Father, Mother, Norman and I boarded the Wacouta in Montreal with Bob Minor, Grandfather's chef from his business car, who looked out for Norman and me in place of Miss Smith [the Slade governess]. We stopped in Quebec for coal, and the village of [Tadoussac] for some sightseeing before anchoring across the reef from St. John. Fortunately, the conditions were good so we took the launch from the Wacouta part way up the St. John where we transferred to canoes and the French guides poled us up the river to the camp seventeen miles from the mouth. I was in the canoe with Grandpa and Grandma. Mother had previously impressed upon me the danger of moving about in a canoe, so I was very still and alarmed to see the guides standing up to pole up the river. When Grandpa stood up, I was terrified! It was late in the season for salmon, but both Mother and Father [took] some.

As the years passed, the next generations of men and women came to fish the river. As always, the guests generally arrived in June and departed in July. They followed the salmon's schedule, arriving when the migration began into the river and leaving when the fish passed out of the property into the upper reaches of the river.

The Next Generations

Gertrude Hill Gavin, James J. Hill's youngest daughter and an avid fisherwoman, was involved in the management of the camp shortly following the death of her father in 1916. Mary (James J. Hill's wife) died in 1921. Gertrude worked closely with Charles Maloney, the camp manager. Maloney was married to the ninth child of Benjamin Chambers Sr. Together, Gertrude and Maloney played an important part in maintaining relationships with the small community on the North Shore. For many years Gertrude kept the accounts and handled the arrangements for the supplies and details of the fishing schedule. She continued the tradition of strong women sports on the St. John River.

In a letter to her sister, Rachel Hill Boeckmann, on January 8, 1942, Gertrude wrote of some of the details involved in keeping the camp in running order, and of the enjoyment she obviously took in fishing the St. John River:

> There is not anything interesting to report about the camp at St. John's River except that starting in 1941 we now have taken up all eight nets at the mouth—having settled with Charles and Raoul Beaudin for $150 each—they had been asking $1000 each.
>
> I have ordered new parts for two outboard motors, and bought a new Johnson Outboard Motor, Model TD, as these things will be almost unobtainable for the next three years [World War II]. For the past year, 1941, there will not be any bill to present. I feel that as you all would have liked to rent the river, and did not try to do so, because of my wanting to fish it, you should not incur the loss of the possible rent and pay out expenses besides. I certainly had enough enjoyment to make it worth my while.

Opposite page, top left: Mary Havemeyer with her seven-fish catch. Mary Havemeyer was Ruth Hill Beard's daughter, born in 1911, and her brother Anson was born in 1909. They were James J. Hill's grandchildren. Anson would eventually manage Hill Camp.

Lower left: Mary Havemeyer with her large fish.

Top right: A quiet moment reveals Gertrude relaxing with her needlepoint on the porch of Hill Camp.

Bottom right: Gertrude stands with two large salmon, and Charlie Maloney (left) and Ben Chambers (right). Home Pool is in the background.

ALL PHOTOS THE FFOLLIOTT FAMILY – MHH COLLECTION

> I should add that the new road has been built to the St. John village. To quote from a letter of Fred Beaudin of October 12, 1941: "On October 11, 1941, the first automobile left Thunder River and came to St. John River by land, on its own power. The road is not finished yet but they are working at it now and they say it will be very good this fall. This means that anyone coming here will be able to land on a wharf at Thunder River and get here with motor cars if the sea is rough on our Bar. This should result in making the trip easier, and the question of guarding against poachers harder."

She signed her letter, "Affectionately, Gertrude."

Great-Grandchildren go fishing

Annually the salmon returned, and they were welcomed as usual. There was no reason for anyone to envision a day when the salmon stock might decline. No one imagined they were overfishing. In Canada and elsewhere in the world, salmon fishers kept on hauling in their prized catches, from boats, in nets and with fly rods. Nature was bountiful and it was not until later, after the war years, that the seriousness of the wild salmon's dwindling numbers would soon be a call for action. This was a beginning of a new direction, a new generation, and a new way of doing things.

Dick (George Richard) Slade is the eldest of the twenty-four individuals who comprise the great-grandchildren of James J. and Mary Hill. James and Mary's third daughter, Charlotte, was Dick Slade's grandmother. In June 1948 Dick made his first visit to Hill Camp and subsequently described what it was like fishing with Gertrude Hill. In the same piece of writing he also reflected on his impressions of his first visit to this remote area, when he was seventeen years old:

From 1940 on, German submarines were spotted in the outer St. Lawrence and within spitting distance of Halifax, Nova Scotia, and the small French islands of Saint Pierre and Miquelon. Those were dangerous and uncertain times in the North Atlantic. By 1942 German U-boats had sunk 198 ships in Canadian waters. They came into the St. Lawrence as far as Rimouski, some three hundred kilometres east from Quebec City. By the end of that year (Sept. 9, 1942), the war cabinet had closed the St. Lawrence to all but local trade. As a result,

Gertrude Hill Gavin, the woman in charge, wearing a hat and tie, with a guide behind her, carrying gear in front of the camp.
PHOTO: THE FFOLLIOTT FAMILY – MHH PERSONAL COLLECTION

the normal activity of river transportation was disrupted and erratic. Servicing the small fishing villages was a very low priority. Younger people of the fishing villages had left for the Canadian Armed Services or to make their contribution by taking well-paying jobs in war industries. Many older residents had died, and the population that had serviced the fishing camps was changed. Consequently, the pre-war routine was abandoned, and a new working order began to emerge by the time I made my first visit to Hill Camp in June 1948.

Clockwise from left: Frank B. Keech, Colonel George T. Slade, Percy Rockefeller, Dr. G.D. Stewart, the seventeen-year-old George Theron Slade, and Anson Beard.
PHOTO: UNKNOWN, 1919 – MHH PERSONAL COLLECTION

View of the "new road" entering the village of St-Jean from the west entrance, showing Highway 138 and the village, with the mouth of the St. John River at the far right. Today it is possible to drive from Montreal to St-Jean.
PHOTO: MARI HILL HARPUR, 2010 – MHH PERSONAL COLLECTION

I was invited to the river by Aunt Gertrude (aka Gertrude Hill Gavin), who was a younger sister to my grandmother Charlotte. At age sixty-four, Gertrude was a New York City resident, a passionate salmon fisherwoman, and probably the driving force behind the other Hill Camp owners.

Aunt Gertrude and her sisters had taken a quasi-maternal interest in my father, Norman, and his sister, Georgiana, as their sister, Charlotte, their mother, had died of cancer in 1923 when she was forty-six years old. Her husband (George Theron Slade) was an avid fisherman and had maintained their access to Hill Camp until his death in 1942.

Our father never had a chance to have the hands-on experience of organizing a trip to the St-Jean, and Gertrude wanted to show her nephew the ropes, so he would see it done right. As it turned out, we were to have a remarkable experience under her watchful glare/eye. Her strong personality and attention to detail shone through every activity at camp. For instance, we were to discover several civilized niceties would appear during our daily routines. They included a written menu describing each meal in the dining room, with a selection of choice wines and an excellent staff working in the kitchen and doing their housekeeping assignments.

But I am getting ahead of myself. That day when we started out for Hill Camp [from Minnesota], Mother drove us to Minneapolis to take the Soo Line overnight sleeper train to Montreal. With me in the car were my father, Norman (then aged forty-five), and my sister, Elizabeth, fifteen. Just two weeks earlier I had graduated from high school and was smugly proud. Our father was wearing clothes that were very familiar to me, from the gray/dark brown fedora, the white striped shirt and tie that he wore in railroad days, work-pants

from his farm wardrobe and dress brown shoes. We sat on the train where time seemed to fly with the miles, and we soon crossed the border into Canada. Our adventure had begun. We stayed one night in Montreal—a metropolis on the verge of rediscovering its French parentage. The following day we boarded the Clarke Steamship Line and headed down the river where we found ourselves docked at Quebec City, a place much smaller, more "historic," and even more French than Montreal. We stopped long enough to gear up at a traditional sporting goods store to purchase the fishing tackle that Aunt Gertrude had thoughtfully ordered by mail. There was only one other guest as I recall, and that was Dr. Birch, Gertrude's physician and great friend from New York City.

Our own gear was fifteen years old and came from my father who had learned about salmon fishing from his father in Norway and the Gaspé peninsula in the 1920s and 30s. His traditional equipment included expensive costumes, hand-tied wet and dry flies, and large but flexible two-handed bamboo poles. The wet flies were double barbed, beautifully tied, and were available in various sizes, most commonly #2, 4, 6, and 8, and in many beautiful colours and patterns. The perfect fly for the early part of the season was the #2. It was big and comparatively heavy, and could handle high dirty water. They sat effortlessly on a rapid current. The slightly smaller #4s and #6s were later-season flies, used in cleaner and clearer water when the river depth had dropped. The others, much smaller flies of 8 and lower, were for the very low water of the second turn and much later in the season. The bigger the fly's number, the smaller the size.

Even as ours was the older generation of tackle, we supplemented our equipment with modern gear. To further prepare ourselves for our fishing

The Côte-Nord and the Innu settlement of Mingan

Margie Gratz, Grace Beek, and Patty Worthing at Harold Chambers's general store

Left to right: Grace Beek, Margie Gratz and Elsi Hill looking at the fish nets drying.

Two children in front of the wood pile.

Mingan dwelling.

Louis and Elsi Hill meet the neighbours.

Photos: Dr. Harvey O. Beek & William Gratz, 1970 – MHH Personal Collection

Local people wait at the dock at Rivière-au-Tonnerre.

Leaving the ferry on a smaller transport boat.

Elsi Hill, Patty Worthing, and Grace Beek.

A special passenger.

Passengers on the ferry.

The Clarke Steamship's Ferry

Photos: Dr. Harvey O. Beek & William Gratz, 1970 – MHH Personal Collection.

Margie Gratz leans against a car while Ludger Chapados and Harold Chambers pose on a truck, and Anselme (Sam) Beaudin (left) and Ernest Chapados stand behind the taxi.

activities, we bought leaders and spare lines. We learned new names: Hardy for flies and tackle, Churchill for reels, and somebody else for the rods. These "houses" came from manufacturers of historic reputation. The rainwear was oilskin with the classic smell and dark colour. We were reminded to get both sunscreen and bug juice because we would be on the river all day, and in the vacant outdoors we would be welcome fresh meat for the bugs. We didn't need to purchase anything else. We were now ready and equipped.

At the Clarke Steamship Company's line, we boarded the ship that would sail that evening. The company ran weekly scheduled ships down the shore from Montreal to farther afield, Prince Edward Island and Newfoundland, before returning the following week. Our view would reveal a wild land with large bluffs along the river's edge. This was an unusual and different territory. Weather permitting, the ship would come into various small settlements and tie up at the pier to unload passengers and their equipage. If the weather were rough, they would unload out in the water onto lighter vessels. The steamer also ran a regular delivery service between villages for the needs of these sparse settlements. Those supplies were critical to their well-being.

At that time the local people fished largely by licensed nets along the St. Lawrence River and up into the feeder streams, while the unlicensed poachers stood constantly at the ready. The poachers were both a social and economic issue in St-Jean and other small villages along the shore. The loss of legitimate and legal practices imperiled the economies of the local villages and likewise for the fishing camps. Farther out on the high seas, deep-netting commercial fishing navies, particularly Scandinavian, had not yet grown into a serious problem. In the near future, as the fish stocks came under pressure by increased fishing, our northern rivers would become a sanctuary for the fish. The rivers served as a relatively secure and private place to breed.

When Elizabeth and I awoke the following morning, we were in the midst of the widening estuary of the St. Lawrence which, had begun to look like an ocean. We arrived at St-Jean in mid-afternoon and were put ashore with our copious baggage. There waited a well-worn Mercury sedan: the local taxi that drove us and our belongings to the landing where the canoes were pulled up along the beach. We stood there in the commotion, surrounded by shouting men and women, a lot of waving of hands, sign language, and confusion, and all in a very different language. Everyone spoke French, and although we could communicate, it was very different for us. We were hustled into the canoes—

The waiting taxi, a 1952 Mercury, would take the guests from the ferry to the canoes to be transported upriver.

Photo: Dr. Harvey O. Beek, 1970 – MHH Personal Collection

Around the Camp

RECIPES

A recipe from Elsi Hill's diary,
dated July 1, 1975:

Asked for filet of salmon for Gravad Lax
& prepared it after lunch:
1/4 c. coarse salt
1/4 c. sugar
Dill
2 tbsp. ground white pepper
It was simple and delicious.

———

A recipe for 'St-Jean Salmon' cooked
over a wood stove from 1988,
taken from Meredith Alden's diary:

- Marinate the salmon fillets from 10-pound fish
  in olive oil, salt, pepper & paprika.
- Then it is covered with a thin layer
  of brown sugar with a sprinkling of lemon
  over the top.
- Rest skin-side down on cardboard
- Place brown or wax paper on top of fish
  for at least four hours.
- Put on a rack & cook over the open flame
  2–2½ minutes on each side in a wire grill.
- Have three pounds of melted butter ready
  & baste the fish all the while it is cooking.
- Test for doneness & skin it.
- Place on platter.

Bon Appétit!

Elsi Hill (left), Dr. Harvey Beek and wife Gracie.

Patty Worthing with Louis Ernest Dérosby (left)
and Raymond Beaudin (right).

Guests sit down for a shore lunch.

The double outhouse: one for men and one for
women, with Grace Beek and Elsi Hill standing.

Patty Worthing under mosquito netting.

"Fish, to taste
right must swim
three times: in
water, in butter,
and in wine."
POLISH PROVERB

PHOTOS: DR. HARVEY O.
BEEK & WILLIAM GRATZ,
1970 – MHH PERSONAL
COLLECTION

some loaded with people and some with baggage. The river's condition was pretty well past the spring overflow, but there were still serious currents and invisible rocks requiring the skill of the guides. This was prior to the time a reliable outboard motor was available. It was still all people-power. The guides would paddle when they could and pole when the water was too shallow or too rapid for security. The guests would sit back, holding tightly to the gunnels, and admire the guides' expertise. We were taken to our great-grandfather's log castle ten miles upriver. We had arrived just ahead of the summer solstice, so we had plenty of daylight. In fact, for our week, which included the longest day of the year, we had not very much darkness even at night.

The following morning after breakfast, we found ourselves on the river: each of us in a sixteen-foot-long canoe going along the currents to our designated pool area. Elizabeth and I fell into our solitary thoughts as we moved through the water, with our boat powered by our guide in the bow and the droppeur (French slang for "he who drops the lead anchor") in the front. The droppeurs were young men who would learn the lore and the river as they worked to qualify as junior guides for less demanding guests. Basically, through their employment, the men worked their way up the prestige (and pay) ladder to become river guides. The guides are storied men who have grown up on the river for generations. They know where the rocks and currents are and how to get into position anywhere in an accessible area to take a fish. This knowledge is not easily acquired.

Some of the camp's guests are legendary. One such icon was President Grover Cleveland, for whom a pool was named not far from the main camp. Family lore says Cleveland was once fishing in Cleveland Pool. He was landing a large salmon when he lost the fish and the rod promptly released its tension. Cleveland suddenly fell heavily into the canoe. He was a large man, obese enough that he awkwardly wedged into the bottom of the boat. The only solution was to pole the canoe to water's edge and have the guides turn the canoe over for the former president to be shaken out! (Family lore also says it was Egil Boeckmann [Hill's son-in law], who was the subject of this "obese glory story." In the end, who knows?) Sometimes information dies with history and sometimes the information is changed, but always there is a little truth in these things. Now, my sister and I were in these same canoes, going to the same places, upriver for our first fishing lesson. I wondered what our moment of glory would be.

On the river, there were several other pools, each with its own personality. One was big enough so that two canoes could fish comfortably. There was another just above the lodge, shared with the leased property owned by the government's camp, called simply The Upper Camp. In those days we fished that pool on alternate days. Then there was another spot, Salt Pool, which was located at the point of the high tide where the salt and fresh water mingled

and the fishing began. At high tide this pool was unfishable, but by low tide it was fine. All guests rotated among the pools going downstream while the fish themselves swam upstream. The pool assignments were day long.

The week that Elizabeth and I were on the river, we would learn to fish with a nine-foot rod, with a reel, and feather fly. Our attempts were focused on the individual specimens rather than full nets. We anticipated finding the tastiest, firmest fish with orange/peachy flesh, bright scales, clear eyes, all fresh from the ocean. We were to hook them just as they swam up the river to lay and fertilize roe and to meet their destinies. We were to rely on our newly developing skills of fishing from a boat that provided a stable platform to give us the ability to cover quite a bit of water while we could see a great distance. Elizabeth and I were delighted to have individual canoes and to be often in sight of each other's rig so that we could see if either of us were having any action. For both of us, this increased the fun of our new skill. It was not long before we experienced firsthand that our flies could distract salmon. So much so that whatever they saw appeared to them to be strange enough to taste. Those fish were so attracted to these floating bits of feathers and metal that they eagerly grabbed the fly with their mouths. Then the game was on!

A lunch break from fishing came at noon. The guests assigned to the lower pools would go ashore to a spot on the high bank that would have been improved with a large shady tent and chairs where the day's picnic and a bottle of beer awaited. The remaining guests who fished the upper pools found it convenient to return to the lodge at noon, where the kitchen would serve a light lunch with wine or beer of choice, after which they might take a nap.

On one particular day, Elizabeth and I were enjoying our streamside picnic at the tent on the lower part of the river. Unbeknownst to us, the lunch at the lodge had taken a turn for the worse. By the time we arrived back at the camp in time for our dinner, we were told the story. The guests' lunch meal, as usual, had been delicious (I still have the menu), and Doctor Birch had eaten well and enjoyed his wine only to get up from the table and collapse as a result of what appeared to be a very serious heart attack. With the help of some staff, my father was able to get him into a bed on the ground floor and make him as comfortable as possible. My father then hastened to retrieve his medical kit, which he had not used for quite some time. After reading the instructional first-aid guide, he reached for the morphine and injected it into the comatose doctor. Messengers raced down to the village, where there was two-way telephone service to Quebec City and the emergency centre at the hospital. The answer came back that we should try to get the doctor to Quebec City as soon as possible. Arrangements were made for flying the still unconscious patient out the next morning via a chartered floatplane that would land at the mouth of the river.

The next day dawned bright, and the older members of the group decided

Time for a Feast!

The accompanying photographs show the use of the wood cookstove used for many years at the camp. Fortunately, this stove has been replaced by a more efficient propane gas oven and stove. The old kitchen was so hot that it was almost impossible to breathe!

Top to bottom, left to right:

Amanda Beaudin-Chambers, 1970.

Ernestine Beaudin at Hill Camp, 1987.

Chef Colette Maloney feeding schoolchildren at the guides' camp, 2001.

Chef Philias (Ti-coq) Beaudin, 1960s.

Chef Edouard Boulet, 1960s.

PHOTOS: UNKNOWN – MHH PERSONAL COLLECTION

Hill Camp 1950s

The women's camp.

The double outhouse.

The main house from the east side.

PHOTOS: DR. HARVEY O. BEEK – MHH PERSONAL COLLECTION

Dr. Birch poses with his morning catch. Birch was a frequent guest of Gertrude Gavin and a great friend who lived and worked in New York City.

PHOTO: THE FFOLLIOTT FAMILY – MHH PERSONAL COLLECTION

that they should leave Elizabeth and me on the river where we could only do harm to salmon. We virtually had the river to ourselves. At about 11 a.m. we saw a canoe coming carefully downstream with the good doctor strapped to the gunnels. I immediately noticed that Dr. Birch was wearing my hand-knit, bright-red hat, the one my sister had knit for me to wear during my "northern adventure." Under these circumstances, it was more appropriate for the doctor to make use of it and also, for us, it was the cheeriest thing in sight. We both stopped fishing, and with the guides dropped our heads in silent prayer.

We stayed out our original plans to catch the Clarke Steamship Company's ship returning to Quebec City in three days' time. This meant three more days of contemplative fishing. Our last day dawned a flat, bright, spring morning, and we left the river in the Village of St-Jean, where the three of us found ourselves in the seat of the same aging Mercury sedan that had served us on the inward journey. We waited for the Clarke Line to come into sight.

What a week this had been! Our father was still in his signature dark fedora, smoking a Camel cigarette, and Elizabeth and I sat thinking about our recent experiences. We looked the same but felt very different. "Well, kids," Pa said, looking at both of us, "what a time we had!" We knew what he thought. Our relationship had changed and matured,

but we had no test to measure this change, only our vibrant memories. We had arrived at camp as children and departed camp as grown-ups. We had spent the days with men who had taught us about the lore of river life. We had experienced something of their lives and emotions. We had battled the salmon, sometimes winning, sometimes losing. We had spent time renewing family ties. We were part of a select group of people who had ventured to Hill Camp. It had proven to be a world of its own. There was no denying it, Elizabeth, Pa, and I had just completed a most unusual ten days of fishing for the Atlantic salmon. Our father was pleased with himself since he had been able to perform admirably for his favourite aunt in responding well to an emergency. In addition, his children, with whom he had sort of lost touch during his wartime absence, had behaved well and fished successfully. Elizabeth and I both set personal bag records for numbers of fish taken and total weight calculated. In gross terms, I took over one hundred fish and weighed in just over a half-ton of salmon. We were bubbling over with new experiences, drama, and happiness in minding manners and re-establishing some of our paternal affections. Aunt Gertrude thought things had turned out very well except for the doctor. The experience had certainly been a success.

Our salmon were in another taxi. They had been kept in the camp's icehouse and had been packed in special wooden crates. Those precious salmon, our trophies, were packed snugly in their wooden coffins. They made it safely all the way back to Saint Paul after having been re-iced in Quebec City and Sudbury, Ontario. As it turned out, Dr. Birch passed away in Quebec City that same week while in the hospital. His last trip was taken in a coffin. He was returned to New York City for his funeral service. All by itself, fly fishing for salmon turned out to be pretty unusual. My last visit to Hill Camp was in 1976, and I believe I killed eighteen salmon, which was not as few as some.

This is an example of the type of floatplane that would have airlifted Dr. Birch from the estuary of the river and delivered him to Quebec City. This particular photograph was taken at a later date, probably around 1953, just below the camp. In any year, however, and even under the best of circumstances, landing a floatplane on this river would have been quite an extraordinary feat.

PHOTO: THE FFOLLIOTT FAMILY – MHH PERSONAL COLLECTION

Playful Times at Hill Camp

A guide holds a salmon above his head in celebration
of the fishing venture.
PHOTO: THE FFOLLIOTT FAMILY – MHH PERSONAL COLLECTION

Jule Hannaford catching a fish. Hannaford had fished the St. John River
with James J. Hill in 1914 and 1915. He was part of Hill's extended
family, and also twice president of the Northern Pacific Railway.
PHOTO: LOUIS W. HILL SR. – MINNESOTA HISTORICAL SOCIETY

Jule Hannaford's daughter in-law, Barbara Hannaford, circa 1960,
wears a flower crown made by Sissy (Mary Boeckmann) ffolliott.
Francis Beaudin is her guide.
PHOTO: THE FFOLLIOTT FAMILY – MHH PERSONAL COLLECTION

Hill Camp was painted red during the late 1950s and early 1960s. The
guides' camp at that time was nothing more than a bunkhouse with a
rudimentary cookhouse. There is a newer women's camp with improved
walkways. A large woodpile covered in plastic waits for colder weather.
PHOTO: MARI HILL HARPUR, CIRCA 1960 – MHH PERSONAL COLLECTION

Anson Beard's Years

Anson Beard Sr. (left) stands with a Portage Pool sign on the lawn of Hill Camp, with Antoine Roussy (middle) and Luc Dérosby (right) and one big fish. The Portage Pool sign indicates the property is privately owned.

PHOTO: UNKNOWN, 1964 – MHH PERSONAL COLLECTION

Anson Sr. in the bathtub before running water was installed. There was no running water or flush toilets at Hill Camp until the late 1970s.

PHOTO: UNKNOWN – MHH PERSONAL COLLECTION

Anson McCook Beard Jr. with his friend Dickey Perkins from Massachusetts, whom Anson has now known for over sixty years.

PHOTO: 1950 – MHH PERSONAL COLLECTION

Anson McCook Beard Jr. is James J. Hill's great-grandson.

PHOTO: MARI HILL HARPUR, 1994 – MHH PERSONAL COLLECTION

The spots on the rock face indicate the water's height in one-foot increments. Observing these two photos you can see that the river height has dropped three feet.

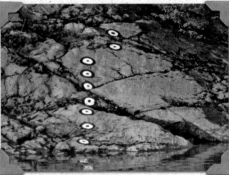

PHOTOS: MARI HILL HARPUR – MHH PERSONAL COLLECTION

Left to right: Marion Hill, my uncle Cortlandt's wife; his older brother, Louis W. Hill jr., my father, standing behind; Andrea Lawrence; Cortlandt Hill; Elsi Hill, my mother; Margie Gratz; Marion Hill in the scarf standing next to their good friends Andrea and David Lawrence.

PHOTO: UNKNOWN – MHH PERSONAL COLLECTION

Changing the Fishing "Turns"

Cortlandt (Corty) and Louis (pronounced Louie) Hill are seen here arriving and departing Hill Camp. They are with their wives and friends, changing their "turn" in front of the house during the 1950s. There was always excitement when someone new came to camp. The camp would buzz with activity, talking, hugging, and kissing, and then tearful goodbyes.

My parents and friends are seen here greeting the new guests accompanying Corty and his wife Marion. With them are Andrea Mead Lawrence with her husband David Lawrence. Corty met the Lawrences when he was the manager of the 1948 and 1952 US ski teams. Andrea was the first woman to win gold for the USA in skiing and later on in her career was the stand-in for Jill Kinmont in the movie *The Other Side of the Mountain*. Corty's son, James J. Hill III, remains good friends with their son today.

As newer generations continued to experience Hill Camp's way of life, the flow of events played out in much the same way as always. James J. Hill's granddaughter, Tudie (Gertrude) Boeckmann ffolliott, enjoyed her long visits to the St. John River. Tudie was a regular visitor and continued to appreciate the sport with her family for many years. For example, from June 29 to July 14, 1974, Tudie fished the river with her husband Peter and two of their children. The Freeman cousins and Jule Hannaford Jr. and his wife were also in the party. That group in 1974 took 138 salmon weighing 612.4 kg (1,350 lbs). The salmon catch was not as prolific as it had been in the past, but the sports' enthusiasm was never lost to the occasion.

As the traditions were passed along to different generations, some practices continued successfully and others were inevitably lost to time. From the 1950s until the 1970s, the fish still migrated through our property, but the quantity of the catch severely declined, and the

special touches at camp, such as handwritten menus, became rare. What remained was the tremendous sense of joy and renewal during every season. At this time, James J. Hill's grandson, Anson Sr., helped his aunt Gertrude as she aged. By the 1950s, Anson had taken over the entire operation and organized the camp with the Chambers family. When Anson's mother Ruth (Gertrude's sister) died in 1959, Anson continued to oversee the operations on the river until 1988. For over forty years, he successfully ran the camp.

Cousin Dick Slade would comment sixty years later:

We saw that the success of the communities adjacent to the river is invariably dependent on the proper management of the salmon camp. It is almost impossible to gauge its importance or put a monetary figure on this value. Honest guides and capable support staff are an essential aspect to a properly run camp. In the little village of St. Jean during the 1950s, the camp's

Gertrude (Tudie) Boeckmann ffolliott with four guides, many fish, and wearing stylish shoes in front of the ice house at Hill Camp, 1933.

Photo: ffolliott Family – MHH Personal Collection

activity provided very welcome cash income for many local families. That income was supplemented by their meagre income from trapping, occasional lumbering, woodcutting, and the public dole. Even today, the men from the town are employed as guides for four to six weeks, and a few others remain at camp doing repairs for a longer period.

Bringing Hill Camp into the modern era had its own challenges. Anson was responsible for re-establishing the record-keeping techniques of his grandfather, which gave the camp a wealth of knowledge about our fish stocks. One of Anson's most lasting legacies was painting the markings on the large granite rock face across from the house. It was Anson who directed the guides to paint the circular target marks with one-foot (0.3-metre) gaps between them. These targets serve as rough indicators of the river's water level. These spots allowed fishers to compare the river's flow and volume over the course of days, even hours. A higher water level means faster waters and the need for heavier flies, while a lower water level can imply slower currents and a call for smaller flies. To this day, guides and guests check the water level first thing in the morning. Often conversations and even friendships begin with a discussion about how many marks show above the water line! Anson was one of the founding members of the Atlantic Salmon Federation, and Anson Jr., his son, continues to be an avid supporter of salmon conservation.

Louis W. Hill Sr. had frequently visited the camp with his father (James J. Hill) and took many of the photographs in this book. He often brought his sons Louis and Cortlandt (Corty) fishing. The sons subsequently divided their father's "time" share of the river (every three years for a week-long stay) between themselves. Various friends and relatives accompanied them on their fishing adventures. There was always a sense of festivity and lighthearted banter amongst the new arrivals.

Women continued to come to the river, adapting to the fishing routine in their own ways. Fortunately for us, during the 1970s and 1980s, several women kept diaries of their visits to the St. John River. Elsi Hill's diary describes the daily rhythm of the camp, much as William Dunwoody's letters had done sixty years earlier. Elsi was my mother, and she loved Hill Camp. She wrote of the pools she fished and the salmon she landed, as well as the fish she lost. Elsi's friends—Meredith Alden, Gladys Ordway, Gracie Beek, Margie Gratz, and Jane Ward Dyer—were often guests of my parents.

Louis Hill Group '60s through '80s

Elsi Fors Hill, streamside in 1959.

Louis W. Hill Jr., with (left to right) Ernest Dérosby, Dalieus Dérosby, Leon Parisee, and Jules Beaudin, behind Héliodore Beaudin, André Beaudin, Lucien Paquet, Raymond Beaudin, and Ludger Chapados, 1970.

Meredith Alden with her first salmon, a two-pound grilse, 1987 – PHOTO: M. ALDEN COLLECTION.

Louis W. Hill Jr., with a lovely prize, 1970.

Colonel Ken Dyer and his wife Jane with three guides: Bertrand Beaudin on right, Jane and Colonel Dyer, Damas Beaudin and Gilles Maloney on far left, 1985.

Gladys and Richard Ordway on camp steps, 1970.

PHOTOS: UNKNOWN – MHH PERSONAL COLLECTION

Elsi and Louis Hill on front steps, 1975.

Guide Dalieus Dérosby takes an afternoon nap in his canoe as he waits for his sport.
PHOTO: UNKNOWN – MHH PERSONAL COLLECTION

Partons, la mer est belle;
Embarquons-nous, pêcheurs,
Guidons notre nacelle,
Ramons avec ardeur.
Aux mâtissons les voiles,
Le ciel est pur et beau;
Je vois briller l'étoile
Qui guide les matelots!

When I came back to camp, I saw Louis had caught a grilse. He believes we should not be keeping the smaller fish. The guides wouldn't let him release it—and neither will Elsi. She says the "guardians," game wardens mainly, told Elsi they are not to release them. Why? They told her they would all be dead anyway. Louis caught another one this afternoon and told me it depressed him to keep them— "What about the future of the river?" he asked of us at dinner that evening. Indeed, that sentiment would become a haunting refrain in its own right.

Day by day, the routine became easier. Damas told me how to place the fly. "Place it only once on either side of the canoe. Take out more line up to the first guide on the rod, then repeat the same thing on the other side of the canoe. Always keep the tip of the rod close to the water. Work the line toward the stern of the boat."

Well, it succeeded! I got my grilse just after letting out more line for the second time, on the second drop. The fish was hooked and he gave me a fine time while the guide and dropdeur *powered the boat to shore. We soon had it netted and if I had been able to release him, I would have for Louis' sake.*

Then my guide grabbed a rock on shore & hit my fish while he was still in the net. John [Meredith's husband] said his guide carries a stick for the purpose that they call a "priest." John also said he's figured it out. "It takes seven hours to catch a fish!" I knew then that I was a lucky sport. Our canoe couldn't have been more proud.

I had a good time. Anyway, I have one fish to my credit. We weigh the fish down at the water, and then we come in. The guide cleaned the fish at a small table right at the front of the stairs to the cabin.

Elsi writes of their enjoyments and accomplishments. Elsi's and Meredith's diaries portray a river that was indeed a "woman's river."

In 1987 and 1988 Meredith Alden describes her own experience while she was a guest of Louis and Elsi Hill. On Saturday June 25, 1988, Meredith writes about her new skill of salmon fishing:

The water is dark; certainly the water is calmer as it glides downstream. On the red rocks which go down to the water's edge there are six white & black targets indicating the height of the river. The conditions were perfect—clear rapid water, sunshine.

I am fishing with Damas (Beaudin); the guide & Carl the droppeur *(he who drops the anchor). We change drops—but in vain: my line had a nice tangle. I have learned to cast better in the process by putting much more line out & I am happy to be able to finish the cast myself. I don't need to have Damas finish the drop anymore. I can cast it out as far as we want, except for these tangles! But never mind, he tells me I am a "bonne pêcheuse."*

Between our fishing drops and, of course, untangling the leader, we spent quite a bit of time singing traditional French-Canadian songs and talking while I cast. There was one song in particular on which we both worked diligently. It is a sad song, but the tune is hauntingly beautiful. Damas comes from a family of French-Canadian troubadours. I can still hear in my mind the eloquent tune as it drifts across the water.

Anselme (Sam) Beaudin cleans a salmon at the beach. Sam had a different way of looking at things. When he spoke, you never knew what to expect. I recall an improvised proverb Sam flung out one day: "*Ah, la pluie qui tombe en masse, un bon jour pour du cabinage.*" ("Oh, the rain is falling so hard, it is a good day to relax in the cabin!") Sam's laughter would often ring out around the camp. He was an orphan who had been left in a basket on the church steps and was brought up by the Sisters. Sam could never read or write, but he had a wonderful disposition, an electric smile, and a wicked sense of humour. He was an excellent fisherman and trapper, and could easily survive alone in the forest.

PHOTO: MARI HILL HARPUR – MHH PERSONAL COLLECTION

Security guards Mark and Matthew patrol the river. PHOTO: MARI HILL HARPUR, 2011 – MHH PERSONAL COLLECTION

On our last day it was such a fine morning. You know there are fish in the black shiny water running on both sides of the canoe—still pools on one side and rocks breaking the other side with rapids. Just trying to put your fly in exactly the right place is fun. We have settled into such a comfortable routine, it's too bad we have to leave tomorrow.

Fortunately for my father, Louis W. Hill Jr., my mother Elsi, a Swede Finn, took to the sport of fly-fishing as if she were born with a rod in her hand. She fell in love with the St. John. Not only was Elsi a superb fisher, she was also an energetic organizer. Her elaborate preparations before every fishing trip could be compared to those made by John Toomey during the early years of Hill Camp. A few months before their arrival at the camp, she would augment her fishing gear and tackle bag by polishing up on her French language skills at a Berlitz school in Minneapolis, Minnesota. She desperately needed to communicate with Harold Chambers and her guide, Louis Ernest Dérosby Sr. Both Louis Jr. and Elsi realized how important it was to maintain the close connections that had been forged with the Chambers family and the local village. Elsi's love for the river is evident in her diary entry of June 30, 1975: "I hope I can retain the beauty, peace & quiet of this river for some time to come."

Elsi's diaries show that her actual planning for the fishing trips began in May and June of the previous year. As had been done since 1900, she took an inventory of what was at the camp and what would be needed for the next visit. By early spring of the fishing season, Elsi had orders and supplies mailed to Harold Chambers (Jean's father and Benjamin Chambers' great-grandson) at St-Jean. She finalized her guest list and scheduled fishing pools and guides, as well as menus. When she arrived at the river, she became the "majordomo" of the camp, making sure all the guests were comfortable and well fed, as well as outfitted for the sport that she so enjoyed, and so enjoyed sharing. She began thinking about the next trip soon after leaving the river.

∞

Poaching is a constant issue at any fishing camp, and Hill Camp is no exception. The first mention of the subject was in a letter that Toomey wrote W. B. D. Scott, manager of the Labrador Company, in July 1907:

We are desirous of having someone who is somewhat familiar with conditions generally at St. John River spend a few days on the river for the purpose of detecting the party or parties who we have reason to believe make a practice of poaching thereon for salmon with nets…

It would be of course expected of the man who would undertake the work to act very discretely and not let it be known by whom he was sent or the purpose he was on the river for and, particularly, not to antagonize any of the people there.

David J. Perrault took on the job of finding the poachers. He was a resident of Quebec and a steamboat captain who sailed vessels on the St. Lawrence River. His "cover" was that he was on the St. John River doing some work with "pulp concerns." Perrault's report to Toomey, on August 20, 1907, reads like a mystery novel:

> Saturday evening I was landed in a dory outside St. John river. The night was very dark and forced us to stay at anchor all night. I took all information I could from the fisherman after I had told them my story about making a survey on St. John harbours to load pulp wood. I learned by these people there was a party of five men fishing salmon up the river. I reached St. John at 4:45 a.m. on Sunday morning and one of Mr. Benjamin Chambers' sons Jim took me to his father's place where I stayed Monday. I started conversation with the old man, Benjamin Chambers, and after having told him the cause of my presence inquired about this party fishing. He told me it was a particular friend of James Hill and two of Chambers's sons (but I knew there was five!). So we kept talking and received a lot of information about pulp wood limits. So, asked if salmon fishing had been any good this summer. He [Benjamin Chambers] told me he had caught eighteen hundred pounds in his right of fishing. [This would have been compliant with Benjamin Chambers's fishing lease, negotiated each year with the government.]

Perrault's letter goes on for thirteen pages, and he narrates his clandestine conversations with the Chambers family members and other St. John men who had nets out for trout (although Perrault is not sure it is trout they are catching). He also discussed this topic with fellow passengers on his trip back to Quebec. By the return trip, Perrault suspects everyone. The conclusion he comes to in his report to Toomey is that there are St. Jean fishermen who are using nets and taking a significant amount of salmon and trout out of the river. He names the people he suspects. In a letter sent to Toomey the next day, August 21, Perrault writes that he spoke to a man who was working for Hill for the last four sseasons, who told him that he had "caught Mr. Benjamin Chambers with his sons fishing salmon during the night with his nets." Toomey's reply to these reports explained to Perrault that the other information sent on was not "definite enough to clearly show whom the party or parties are who may have been poaching on the St. John River." There is no documentation supporting how the suspected poaching was resolved.

A river guard with his basset hound.
PHOTO: MARI HILL HARPUR, 2000 – MHH PERSONAL COLLECTION

Security on a River

One of the more challenging aspects of salmon-river management is controlling the illegal disruption of fish habitat. In our waters it has been necessary to engage security guards to patrol the river system during the fish's active season (April to October). Here, they are photographed at the beginning of their night patrol. This photograph was taken in the vicinity of where a poacher's body had been discovered two years previously. It was a tragic story. Sadly, it seems that the poacher fell out of his canoe, became entangled in his own net, and drowned.

A canine river guard. A dog in the canoe waits for the evening shift.
PHOTO: MARI HILL HARPUR, 2011 – MHH PERSONAL COLLECTION

Preparing for the New Millennium

The next generation to manage the camp at the St. John River was led by me, Mari Hill, James J. Hill's great-granddaughter. I had first visited Hill Camp at the age of fifteen with my parents; I was also introduced to Jean Chambers and his twin brother Gilles (great-grandchildren of Benjamin Chambers Sr.), who were a year older than me. They made my first Hill Camp visit really fun and helped to introduce me to the river's ways. I did not realize it then, but it was I who was hooked, not the fish. At that time, I had no way of knowing that I would return to the camp for many years to come to enjoy our river world. What was then a school holiday would turn out to be a lifelong commitment to the King of Sport.

I recall that the 1980s brought some hardships to the river. Family members were having difficulty coping with the modern and off-site management. Occasionally illness and advanced age interfered. Sometimes events happened that were somewhat out of the norm. In 1982 my mother and her close friend Gladys Ordway were at the camp alone. My father and Gladys' husband Dick were both ill and under a doctor's supervision in Minnesota. While their husbands were unable to travel, Elsi and Gladys decided to go to Hill Camp as planned. After all, the visit was only for a week, and everything was already set for their arrival. They were there during the Quebec national holiday, St-Jean-Baptiste Day, June 24.

This is the traditional holiday of Quebec culture. According to tradition, all up and down the coast the villagers set large fires along the shore to celebrate this night. They are honouring St. John the Baptist, who is the patron saint of Quebec and represents Quebec cultural heritage. The very first St-Jean-Baptiste celebrations were said to have taken place on the banks of the St. Lawrence River on the evening of June 23, 1636. A bonfire and five cannon shots accompanied their festivities. Flashing forward 376 years, what ordinarily would have been a joyful celebration turned into a terrifying ordeal for the two older women at Hill Camp. In the dark hours of the morning a group of local celebrants arrived on their all-terrain vehicles, and lit a large bonfire at the river's edge across from the house. Those nocturnal visitors proceeded to fire gunshots at the *grande maison*. Except for a few holes in the roof, there was no damage. Luckily, no one had access to the cannon that had been in use in 1636, otherwise this incident might have had a much different ending!

The *Côte-Nord* has other reputations, especially for song and poetry. One of the more famous residents is from Natashquan: the nationalist icon, singer Gilles Vigneault. Similar to others who have visited the area, the poets and singers of Hill Camp have called on their imaginations to describe their fishing experiences.

Our daughter Sara Maud won a school prize for the following poem she composed in 1993:

> *Morning layers of white haze*
> *Swirl down the Saint Jean,*
> *Nuzzling the fallen pines & the ruby-grey clay*
> *That decorate its steep banks.*
>
> *Tousled clouds shuffle along the northern sky,*
> *As I strategically place*
> *The alluring fly into the rocky pool.*
> *Methodically I place the line &*
> *My sundial shape is completed.*
>
> *Scrutinizing the waters' winking surface,*
> *I discern the lazy clouds, the blueing sky,*
> *Hopefully the salmon's tail.*

Everyone who comes to the camp adds his or her own touch to its mosaic. Louis and Elsi Hill continued to maintain the river so that Hill Camp would be handed down to the next generation of friends and sports. But the modern dynamic was unfolding in ways that would change traditional camp life. In 1987, not long after the fishing season was over, I was reminded of my father's earlier sentiment that he had shared in numerous conversations with Meredith Alden: "What about the future of the salmon and the river?"

Family days in camp

Me at age fifteen with my guide,
Gadias Paquet.
PHOTO: UNKNOWN, 1964 –
MHH PERSONAL COLLECTION

Me with Elsi and
Louis, my parents.
PHOTO: UNKNOWN –
MHH PERSONAL COLLECTION

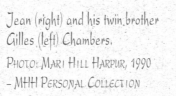

Jean (right) and his twin brother
Gilles (left) Chambers.
PHOTO: MARI HILL HARPUR, 1990
– MHH PERSONAL COLLECTION

Left to right: James J. Hill III,
me, and Doug Harpur.
PHOTO: UNKNOWN, 2001 –
.MHH PERSONAL COLLECTION

Stepping Lightly into the Future

During the late 1980s, the decline of the Atlantic salmon catch on our river and other Maritime rivers was alarming. There was a substantially lower salmon count than in the previous years. We did not know why things were becoming more difficult for the health of the salmon, but we knew we somehow had to help them. We needed to make some hard decisions, and we needed to understand more about fish habitat. We wanted to modify the manner in which we operated the camp. But how? Little by little, our plan started to formalize. This is how it all began.

It was late on a Friday afternoon in the summer of 1986 when my office phone rang. I answered the phone and spoke with a man who introduced himself as a lawyer from Sept-Îles, Quebec. I knew immediately that it had something to do with Hill Camp. He had my full attention. He politely told me that our property on the west side of the river was to be sold the following Monday for the amount of back taxes owing, and that parcel of land included the buildings and the house! Since I had recently taken over the management of Hill Camp from my uncle, Anson Beard Sr., I was not surprised that something had been missed during our transition, but this news was very dramatic and required immediate attention. From that moment on, I became focused on the camp's management. I remember hanging up the telephone and going into the adjoining office. There was my husband Doug and our lawyer Robert (Bob) Smith. I said, "Since you two are so smart, tell me how to buy a salmon river!"

Bob's ears immediately perked up. "A salmon river! That sounds interesting. Tell me more, Mari." And so it began. From then on, we were on track to having better control of our river.

After taking care of the back taxes, we decided to reorganize the ownership structure of Hill Camp. During the ensuing months, Bob, Doug, and I developed a fair proposal. We imagined an agreement that would appeal to all remaining family owners. We had Uncle Anson's appraisal, which he had commissioned several years earlier. We knew the task ahead of us would not be easy, and in retrospect I realize I had taken on something larger than I knew. Our proposed course of action would involve a lot of participants, and I had to manage not one thing but a multitude of variables. Fortunately, I was young and luckily I inherited my

In 1995 Sara Maud became a guide and could drive the canoes anywhere along the river. Quite an achievement for the first woman guide at Hill Camp!
PHOTO: MARI HILL HARPUR – MHH PERSONAL COLLECTION

great-grandfather's genes. I invited many of my professional friends to come fishing, and during those long discussions we brainstormed about the camp.

Our first stop would be with Uncle Anson. We needed to agree on a price per share (or ownership units), which I would then present to the remaining owners. I would ask them to make one decision: stay involved in Hill Camp financially or be paid out.

Sara Maud was soon to be on her school's spring break. I needed her support and arranged to meet Uncle Anson during her vacation. So, together, Sara Maud and I left for Anson's hometown of New York City. On the plane from Montreal we carried a brand new portable Hewlett Packard laptop with its own dedicated printer; it was one of the first of its kind sold in Canada. The only file on that computer was the offer to purchase the shares of Hill Camp. Sara Maud and I spent that night with Rosanne, Anson's wife, in their city apartment. She was a lovely, tall, charming, and imposing woman. Dinner was appropriately at the Colony Club on Park Avenue. The club had been founded in 1903 as a women-only private club. It would have hosted many of the wives and daughters of James J. Hill's fellow fishermen and business associates. The feeling of the turn-of-the-century interior

Elsi at left, next to Mari and Sara Maud 1987.

carried us through the morning's discussions. It was as if we were fishing: one cast here, a small take there, while we waited for a rise to the dancing fly. Back and forth we cast our lines. I thought of my father's favourite fly, the blue charm. There we three were, sitting, trying to be charming, certain that our price had to be honest and fair for all of us. Finally, Rosanne came to the rescue. She had been silent, listening to our conversation from the adjoining room. I heard her chair slide across the floor. She entered the room and stood with her arms folded across her chest, leaning against the doorframe, and said, "Will you please make up your minds so we can have lunch and a drink!" Sara Maud looked at me while I looked at Anson. We had been stuck on two contradictory figures for about an hour. Neither of us would budge. I thought of the

design and elaborate place settings reminded us of the opulence of the golden age of clubs and fishing camps. Back in 1903, the fee to join the Colony Club was $150, with $100 annual dues. But there Sara Maud and I were sitting together with thoughts of the deal at hand surrounded by the ghosts of ages past. In some ways, being family would be the only ticket we needed to accomplish our task.

The following morning, Rosanne had her car brought around—a big, plush car, which she drove very fast. In the early morning mist, we hit all the green lights on Park Avenue and soon left the city in our wake. New York's pace was certainly a far cry from that of the St. John River!

When we arrived at their home, Uncle Anson received us with his usual dignity and charm. Without beating around the bush, we cut to the main topic: what was the value per share? That figure, at best, was a moving target and would prove to be hopelessly elusive. We had purposely left a glaring blank space in the agreement for the price. For a while, the conversation did not go so well. Dialogue, as always with Uncle Anson, was easy, but it was taking time to establish a workable price. We were all striving for mutual agreement and good will. Our good intentions and congeniality

Me (right) and my daughter Sara Maud sitting on the camp porch.

blue charm again, and I offered to raise my price per unit to get closer to the one he was willing to accept. Although we had not discussed this, Sara Maud turned to me with a look of disgust and said, as if on cue, "Dad said not to go that high." It was perfect. Uncle Anson looked at Sara Maud, then back at me. "Give me the pen." It happened just like that. Anson felt he had the best deal he was going to get, while we agreed and signed the document. Anson had his life back, Sara and I had our agreement, and Rosanne served lunch.

∞

By September 1988, Doug and I had successfully reorganized the camp's management structure into Club Hill Camp, Inc. Now we were going strong as we entered the modern era. We did not foresee it at the time, but at that point we were sitting in the canoe and about to go down the rapids full speed ahead!

The 1990s proved to be a particularly violent chapter in the camp's history. There is still a file in our office labelled "Salmon Wars," and at that time it was an appropriate title. The war started slowly and gradually picked up momentum. During that decade, the provincial government reorganized its method of controlling river leases across the province by discontinuing the majority of the current leasing agreements, some of which had been in place for many years. In French slang, this campaign was known as the *déclubage des rivières*. Unfortunately, misunderstanding and mistrust followed this decision. Many people did not appreciate what was taking place. As a result, many of the rivers became targets for overfishing, illegal fishing, trespassing, and even vandalism.

It was early in the season of 1991. At Upper Camp, the government had cancelled the previous lease, which had been in place for over fifty years, held by a prominent conservationist and sportsman, Daniel M. Galbraith, of Pittsburgh. After a lot of lobbying and coercion, a local group from the village of St-Jean had formed a cooperative and had been given the lease on the upper part of the river, running from our property line and north to the 30 Mile Falls. This local population, which had little notion of private ownership rights, was determined to get possession of the entire river for their own use. They announced by phone and newspaper that there would be public fishing on our part of the river. To emphasize their point, they organized a protest for St-Jean-Baptiste Day. There were rumours of two hundred boats

Louis and Elsi Hill at the lawyer's office in Montreal, September 1988.
PHOTO: MARI HILL HARPUR, SEPTEMBER 1988 – MHH PERSONAL COLLECTION

coming to the river that day in support of the locals. Leading up to the weekend, there were men and women trawling for fish with all types of gear and disturbing our waters. They were aggressive, though not violent, and they did everything in their power to prevent us from taking up our regular fishing routine.

As luck would have it, we had rented the river for the following week. There was no way we were going to let our guests be harassed. I resumed my plans to immediately return to Montreal while Doug and Jean were consulting with the local police. They did not want to get involved in fishing rights, but Doug and Jean understood the seriousness of the situation. They were arranging to hire sixteen Pinkerton guards to fly in from Baie-Comeau to help secure the river and protect our guests. The police begged them not bring in the guards, as they felt this was going to lead to violence. Finally the police agreed to monitor and patrol the river. They assured us they would be a presence on the river and deal with safety issues and other infractions. They agreed to put two officers at the southern end of our property, another two at the north end, and a patrol boat on the river. By the end of the day, they had issued a multitude of infractions dealing with everything from alcohol in boats to oversized motors and various safety issues. From that day forward we engaged professional river guards to monitor the use of our ownership.

The harassment continued for another two or three years. In the interim we agreed to let residents of the village of St-Jean fish a lower part of the river we were not using. The residents had to sign an agreement and pay a nominal fee. Unfortunately there were a few individuals who continued to cause trouble on the river. Several names were presented to the local judge, who in turn granted us an injunction to stop those selected people from harassing us. The police could now charge them with disturbing the peace. The war was over. Fortunately, the proceedings played out without harm or violence. Calm was eventually restored. A normal life resumed along the river, and once again fish and fishing were the primary subjects of conversations and poetry.

Canoes along the beach at the end of the day in the evening light.
PHOTO: MARI HILL HARPUR — MHH PERSONAL COLLECTION

Chapter Six

From Recreation to Resource Management

(1989 – 2012)

Hill Camp pin in green, designed
by Anson Beard Sr. in the 1950s.

PHOTO: MARI HILL HARPUR – MHH PERSONAL COLLECTION

Hill Camp pin in blue, designed by James J. Hill III
as a centennial celebratory pin in 2003.

PHOTO: MARI HILL HARPUR – MHH PERSONAL COLLECTION

Jocelyn (Tintin) Beaudin at Hill Camp,
ferrying across the river with a canoe.

PHOTO: MARI HILL HARPUR – MHH PERSONAL COLLECTION

"No matter what road I travel, I'm going home."

— Shinsho, Japanese Shinto monk proverb

The New Millennium: Centennial Observations and the Science of it All

North Atlantic salmon may venture into the world, but they always return to their home river system to spawn. Just as the salmon return home, so do the guests at Hill Camp. By 2001, Hill Camp had made it through its first century (1901 – 2001), and the beautiful log homestead had survived intact. For us, the new millennium arrived without too much fanfare. Celebrations for Hill Camp's first one hundred years actually took place in 2003. Our festivities were not elaborate, but all who attended camp that year felt the impact of history. The camp had lasted into the new millennium, and we possessed the means and desire to protect and prepare our river for future *Salmo salar* generations. We were about to launch ourselves into a wonderful world of primary research at the riverside.

Previously, our river had little human disturbances, being isolated by single-road access. Along its banks, canoes, with their small 9.9 hp motors, were the main form of transport for the two camps. Today, during the winter months, there are different visitors pushing their way along the frozen river and into the vast interior. Winter and summer boulevards for Skidoo and four-wheeler traffic traverse the landscape. Coincidently, over the last three decades, there has also been a marked decline in the North Atlantic salmon population.

Our goal was simple. We wanted to establish a way of monitoring the health and status of the *Salmo salar* population of the St. John River. Ideally, we wanted to find an acceptable and workable methodology that would let us estimate both the number of smolts leaving the river for the first time on their feeding journey to the sea, and the number of adults returning from the sea to the river to spawn. We also wanted an index of the numbers and growth of the juvenile salmon (parr) that stayed in the river for up to five years after they hatched from their eggs before making their fateful journey to the sea. Our data is collected to help articulate our future conservation practices. St. John River salmon were also incorporated into a pioneering new study of the ocean life of Atlantic salmon. Both smolts and adult salmon were fitted with acoustic tags, and their movements in the river and across the Gulf of St. Lawrence toward their ocean feeding pastures were captured as the animals moved past moored acoustic receivers lying in wait to detect their passage.

Establishing a river-specific watershed management program on the St. John was not an easy task. One of the hardest jobs is actually catching salmon for the scientific work, and here there was a natural role for the anglers frequenting Hill Camp. Our angler-based research program began to take shape in 1998. It would take months of preparation, but we finally agreed to four objectives for the program. We decided to:

Doug Harpur, my husband, guiding Hill Camp into the new millennium. Club Hill Camp was brought into the modern era largely through the direction and effort of T. R. Douglas Harpur, who oversaw the entity's corporate restructuring and helped develop a scientific research program as an effective way to manage the St. John's ecosystem, in 2009.
PHOTO: MARI HILL HARPUR, 1999 – MHH PERSONAL COLLECTION

1. Establish an annual population estimate for the adult salmon run through a mark-capture methodology executed on fish caught by the sports and anglers through live captures;
2. Monitor the juvenile salmon population;
3. Document the temperature regime of the river; and
4. Work with local schools to familiarize students with their backyard ecosystems.

These studies were intended to document the current health of the river's salmon population, as well as provide new knowledge about where smolts and adult salmon go. The work would describe the salmon's critical habitat and feeding areas, especially in the St. John River. Additionally, we were concerned with the impact of predators, including birds, seals, and humans. Out of some eight thousand eggs laid and naturally fertilized, only two adult fish will survive to spawn again. We wanted to discover when, where, and how the *Salmo salar*'s mortality occurs.

These seemed like ominous goals to me. Never good at science and not having had much exposure to primary research, I was in the dark about what all of this would mean for the river, for the camp, and for our lives. Fortunately, I was not alone. My husband

From left to right: Research assistant Jean Carreau, guest Dr. Corrin Hodgson from Rochester, Minnesota, and Dr. Roger Buckland of McGill University, Montreal, Quebec.
PHOTO: MARI HILL HARPUR, 1999 – MHH PERSONAL COLLECTION

Doug and I benefited from the influence of Doug's parents, both of whom were doctors and biochemists, and with our hands-on business interests in farming and forestry, we embraced the project wholeheartedly. We began to assemble our team. Dr. Fred Whoriskey, who was then leading the research at the Atlantic Salmon Federation in St. Andrews, New Brunswick, spearheaded our program. We also collaborated with McGill University, represented by the Dean of Macdonald Campus, Dr. Roger Buckland. When these professionals were in place we worked to establish a relationship with the Quebec government. We contacted the provincial authorities to address compliance issues and get the necessary permits to conduct the research. As soon as we could establish a productive routine that had the government's approval, we would need to gather the people who would implement the program and maintain the statistics. We were finally headed in the right direction.

Dr. Buckland, a keen fisherman, went to the oldest sail-making company in Montreal and with them helped design and manufacture the *panier pour le canot*, a watertight basket that can be filled with river water and held across the canoe gunnels by wooden dowels. The live-capture protocol for angled adult salmon was starting to materialize. We intended to catch the salmon in the river, place the fish in the *panier*, remove the fly from the salmon's mouth, measure its length, take a scale sample, and insert an external tag at the base of its dorsal fin. Afterward, we would safely return the fish back into the river. Dr. Buckland was able to locate a student in biology who would serve as the on-site operator and coordinate with Dr. Whoriskey. Meanwhile, several biologists from the Quebec government through the Société de la faune were communicating with us, too. The government owned the property north of us. We called on Upper Camp to enlist their participation as an additional location site for the program.

At the beginning of the project we used techniques that had not been attempted before, especially on large rivers like the St. John. In 2000, we installed a weir across the river that was supposed to direct the salmon into a counting cage. With this contraption, we intended to inventory the number of adult fish that swam up the river. Unfortunately, this was not a success. With the combination of the weather and strong currents in the river, the migrating salmon always managed to find a way upstream, avoiding the trap.

However, we did have some early initiatives that were successful. In one of the projects, which was very enjoyable for all involved, local elementary-school students assisted in raising juvenile salmon from the egg stage to the smolt stage in an aquarium in their classroom during the winter term. The following June, the students arrived at the camp with Dr. Whoriskey and released the smolts into the river. Jean Chambers was on site and gave them a tour of the house, including an animated talk about the historical objects that adorn the house's walls. They ate their lunch in the guides' camp before returning to Longue-Pointe-de-Mingan. What a crowd of happy and switched-on kids!

On June 27 of that same year, the river was all abuzz with a story of a different twist. That morning, a local angler from the village of St-Jean had been fishing in Salt Pool. He never realized how hot the competition could become. A loon flew overhead and quickly swerved down and took his fly. The angler tugged and tugged, and the loon fought and fought. Andy Moss, then the resident researcher, rushed to help. Both men pulled the line so hard that the leader broke and the loon flew away. If you fish long enough, you will see it all.

In 2001 we began our electrofishing study, which was an intricate and important part of our research. The information was used to monitor fry and parr densities in six areas of the St. John

Dr. Fred Whoriskey (left) and Jean Chambers (middle) oversee the release of smolt with schoolchildren.
PHOTO: MARI HILL HARPUR, 2001 – MHH PERSONAL COLLECTION

Gino Doucette (right) and Mike Martin sampling smolt by electrofishing.
PHOTO: MARI HILL HARPUR, 2001 – MHH PERSONAL COLLECTION

River system on a yearly basis. The electrofisher, a backpack-sized device used by biologist Gino Doucette, gives out a short burst of electricity into a small area of the river. This renders the tiny fish within range of the electrical field unconscious for a short time. The stunned fish are then collected for additional study. Mike Martin, a student at the University of New Brunswick, assisted in 2001, followed by Scott Flash the following year. Information obtained from the sampled fish included ages from scale samples, weights, lengths, and various other data. When combined with the numbers of fish captured at the sites annually, the results paint a picture of how the juvenile salmon numbers in the lower river were trending over time. In essence, the data provided a kind of early-warning system of what we might expect for smolt output from the river.

When we started an adult tagging program that same year, we initially used Floy plastic tags. The combined expertise of the guide and the angler allowed the small plastic tag to be inserted into the upper portion of the fish's body, at the base of the dorsal fin where the tag could be securely anchored. This occurred directly after the fish was angled and just before it was released. The hope was that we would be able to mark and recapture a sufficient number of salmon to develop a reliable population estimate for the number of salmon in the river as an alternative to the failed trap net. Unfortunately, we were unable to mark and recapture sufficient numbers of salmon to accomplish the goal. Because of the low recapture rate, this tagging program was discontinued in subsequent years. During the year the program was in force, out of the twenty-one fish tagged, only one was recaptured, by angler Sara Maud Vanier, James J. Hill's great-great-granddaughter. The first recapture occurred on the morning of June 28, by Sara Maud and Yoland Beaudin in Portage Pool with a Rusty Rat #6. Fourteen days previously (June 14, tag # 03101), that same fish had been caught and tagged by Dr. Roger Buckland in Home Pool with a Grizzly King #4. In her fishing report from that season, Sara Maud wrote: "All in all, the river seemed to be teeming with silver-bodied fish. It was the most exciting news; proof of a capture of a previously caught salmon! Very exciting! So now we can scientifically prove that the salmon survive the tagging."

Undaunted, we continued our studies of the adult fish by measuring the length of the fish's body and, when possible, collecting scales for aging of the angled and released fish. We processed all harvested fish, collecting similar information to that which we acquired from the electro-fished juveniles: weight, sex, scale aging, and DNA (from tissue samples). Observing a scale under a microscope and analyzing the pattern of ring deposition (like tree rings) is the way a fish's age is determined. In addition, calcium reabsorption marks on the scales of adults indicate how many times an individual fish has returned to the river as an adult to spawn. These marks occur because the adult salmon do not feed in rivers for six months or more once they arrive for spawning. Instead, they absorb stored body nutrients to survive, including some of the calcium in their scales.

Reading the Rings in Salmon Scales

This image was taken after the scale sample was removed from the salmon and placed on a tape to be preserved in our data bank.

Photo: Mari Hill Harpur – MHH Personal Collection

The age of a wild salmon can only be determined by reading the scale of a wild salmon through a microscope. The fish's age is determined by counting each winter it stayed in fresh water, represented by the smaller rings (annuli) seen in the centre of the scale. The small spaces between the annuli are caused by slow growth in winter conditions. Larger spaces between the annuli are caused by the summer growth created by the abundance of food in the open oceans. Similar to the rings of a tree, one tight ring equals one year spent in the river, where the fish do not eat. Once the smolt heads to sea, it feeds constantly from six months to three years of age. This represents one "sea winter." This method of determining age cannot be applied to farmed salmon since they have a constant food source available.

A salmon scale showing ring marks.

Photo: Dr. Fred Whoriskey Collection, Halifax, Nova Scotia

Annabel Wallis (left) of Wanaka, New Zealand visits the smolt wheel with Gino Doucette.

PHOTO: MARI HILL HARPUR, 2003 – MHH PERSONAL COLLECTION

A smolt wheel is comprised of a stationary, rotary, screw drum that rotates by the force of the river's current. The apparatus is installed on top of a catamaran platform that supports the rotating drum and filters the water while funnelling principally live smolts, as well as small numbers of parr and other species of small fish safely into a holding chamber. Every morning all fish captured during the previous twenty-four hours were processed and recorded, and Gino Doucette, the resident biologist, attached an adipose fin clip. The clipping was done to attempt to estimate the river's annual smolt run using a mark recapture estimate. Clipped fish were released upstream of the wheel, where they mixed with unmarked fish. In addition, the daily capture rates of smolts could be correlated to environmental conditions, such as temperature and water velocity. As well, the timing of the annual smolt run could be fully documented and compared to patterns in other years to see if systematic changes were occurring, perhaps associated with climate change. In 2003, the year the apparatus was installed, 360 smolts were captured in the smolt wheel, which included the five

that were recaptured as indicated by the marking on their fins. Additionally, a total of sixty-nine salmon parr were taken, forty-three brook trout (*Salvelinus fontinalis*), twenty-four American eels (*Anguilla rostrata*), ten three-spined stickleback (*Gasterosteus aculeatus*), twenty-seven lamprey (*Petromyzon marinus*), and fifty-four lake chub (*Couesius plumbeus*), along with one white sucker (*Catastomus commersoni*). Annually, the smolt wheel was in operation for approximately one month.

The results of the 2005 field season were even more exciting, because of the instigation of an acoustic (sonic) telemetry initiative, a tracking system made especially for marine animals. This part of the study was to include both adult salmon and smolts. Our river was the most northern in a series of Gulf of St. Lawrence rivers included in the study, with the others located in Canada's Maritime provinces. At last we were part of a bigger network, which ranged from our river as the northern boundary to the southernmost point in New Brunswick. (The research rivers from south to north where tagging occurred were the Magaguadavic, the Miramichi, the Restigouche

106 – SEA WINTER SALMON

(our old friend from the early Lord Stephen's days with James J. Hill; see Chapter Three), the Cascapédia, and the St. John. This spread of watersheds represents a 660-kilometre, north-to-south cline.)

During 2005 at Hill Camp, two adult salmon were fitted with sonic tags by a surgical procedure, and in subsequent years additional adults and smolts were tagged. The smolt tags were 20 x 9 mm (0.7 x 0.35 in) and adult salmon tags were 65 x 9 mm (2.5 x 0.35 in). The batteries in the smolt tags have a life of about seventy days, while the larger adult tags last for approximately four hundred days. The tags were inserted in the fish's abdominal cavity and the wound sealed with stitches. During the time of surgery, the fish are anaesthetized, and their gills are irrigated to provide oxygen. After recuperating in a holding tank in the river, the fish are released to continue their migration. Within the river, twelve receivers tracked their progress. It was noted that both these adult fish in 2005 eventually continued upstream toward the spawning beds. It took them twelve to thirteen days to reach the waterfall at the 30 Mile Pool. Meanwhile, back in the smolt study, ten smolts were tagged and successfully tracked as they moved out of the river in the Gulf of St. Lawrence. The estimated survival rate from smolt to adult salmon in some of the North Shore rivers monitored by Faune and Parcs Québec was now about 1 percent. Clearly more information was needed about the salmon's life at sea.

During the 2006 season, ten adult fish were tagged and 8 of them were detected above 30 Mile Falls in July. These adult salmon navigated the 18 kilometres (11 miles) from the river and its estuary to Hill Camp in an astounding river transit time ranging between 14 hours 22 minutes to 54 hours 6 minutes. Speedy fellows, considering their size and also considering their metabolism had to adjust from the salt-water environment to fresh water!

Additionally, the two adult fish that were tagged in the summer of 2005 were detected as "kelts"—locally named "black fish," or "slink"—the following year. These "black fish" are the adult fish that entered the river as fresh adults the previous year to spawn, remained in the river system, successfully lived through the winter, and have begun a return migration to sea in the following spring. They represent the river's strongest genetic stock, since they are clearly survivors. These two black fish were detected moving downstream in early spring 2006, successfully swimming through the estuary, where they were expected to enter the St. Lawrence River in May or early June, before the returning ocean fish arrived.

An unusual occurrence happened in 2006 when two fish "disappeared" from all of our river's receivers! A possible explanation for the loss of their signals was that the fish and their tags were removed from the water by either an aerial or terrestrial predator, or a poacher, although it was possible that they somehow slipped by the receivers without being detected.

Only one of the two fish that disappeared was detected the following year when new data was retrieved from the receiving unit. So the lost fish was our first scientific evidence of one salmon's mortality.

Guide Alexandre Cauchy Richer from the Quebec area poses with a "black fish" about to be released. Notice how long and slim this fish is. This fish has not eaten for the year he has been living in the river.

PHOTO: MARI HILL HARPUR, 2013 – MHH PERSONAL COLLECTION

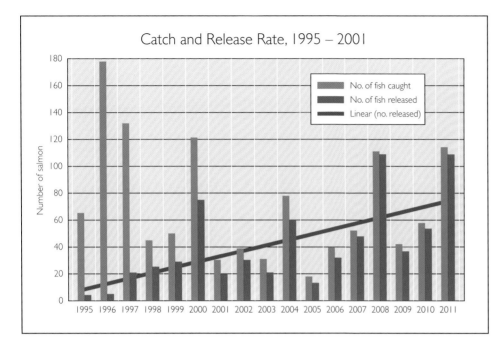

Catch and Release Rate, 1995 – 2001

Number of salmon

- No. of fish caught
- No. of fish released
- Linear (no. released)

Statistical analyses of Hill Camp catch and release rate, 1995 – 2011

temperature at no time exceeded the 23°C temperature threshold at which catch-and-release fish begin to suffer mortality. It is also the correct temperature for optimum sustainability. Specifically, the temperature recorded on May 26, 2006, was 9.3°C (48.7°F) and the maximum recorded was on July 20, 2006, 22.1°C (71.7°F). By July 19, all tagged fish were above the waterfall. This was the biological closing of the salmon-angling season for that year.

After the successful fishing season of 2006, our research area took in an even greater scope. In the Strait of Belle Isle—the Gulf of St. Lawrence's northernmost exit to the Atlantic Ocean, located between Newfoundland and Labrador—twenty-two acoustic receivers were installed on the buoys that span the channel. These receivers were placed as a "gate" to detect fish moving through this passage into the Atlantic Ocean. Hill Camp research had reached out way beyond its original boundary.

Our telemetry studies also indicated conclusive proof that catch and release, done properly, is successful and does not impede the migratory progress of the fish's life pattern. Since the start of our research, the catch and release rate at Hill Camp has been around seventy-five percent, while that of our northern neighbour, the Pourvoirie de la Haute St-Jean, is around eleven percent released adult salmon. By 2006 the Hill Camp catch and release rate had increased to eighty percent.

In the smolt study, we were beginning to collect a fairly large amount of data. A total of 254 smolts were captured and of those, twenty-six of the thirty tagged smolts survived the 18-kilometre (11-mile) trip to the sea to continue to the Gulf of St. Lawrence. The average smolt movement was 10 kilometres (6.2 miles) per day. Juvenile densities have remained consistent with levels that we have seen since we first began studying their population. Now we could realistically contemplate what was happening to those little smolts!

The river's habitat seemed in good physical shape, a healthy and nurturing environment for salmon. The maximum water

Graph of statistical analysis of historic seasonal catch and effort comparison

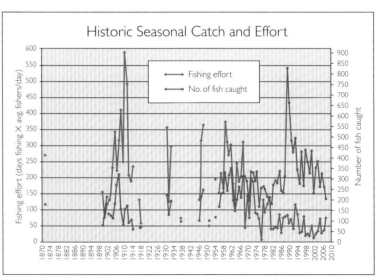

Historic Seasonal Catch and Effort

Fishing effort (days fishing X avg. fishers/day)

Number of fish caught

- Fishing effort
- No. of fish caught

Doug Harpur (right), Dr. Fred Whoriskey, and Marylise Lefèvre (left) discuss their research project while walking along the Gulf of St. Lawrence at the St. John River estuary below Robin's Point.

PHOTO: MARI HILL HARPUR, 2007 — MHH PERSONAL COLLECTION

As we continued our research, we learned an enormous amount. The next six years went by quickly. We fine-tuned the procedures and adopted emerging technology as it became available. We eventually incorporated acoustic tagging of the smolts from our capture wheel, and the St. John's salmon became statistics in the wider arena of oceanographic monitoring. The research results were also reported annually to provincial wildlife biologists and were used in the compilation of the annual "state of the salmon" for the province of Quebec.

During the years of our research journey (2000 – 2012), six biology students assisted the program. Working together, we documented many facts about the salmon's life cycle that until recently had only been supported by educated guesswork. All of our primary research pointed to the salmon's continued survival, and season by season we began to understand their bigger world. The result of our years of tests and recorded information has given us indicators of the health of the St. John River salmon and a glimpse into the fish's personal lives. Our research helped determine the approximate population density in the St. John and also to identify some of the salmon's migration pathways to their feeding grounds.

Marylise Lefevre spent five years (2006–2011) administrating our streamside research project. It was normal to see Marylise snorkelling along the riverbank observing habitat at close range. In 2012 Marylise described her research experience on the St. John River:

The Rivière St-Jean offers a pristine habitat for the wild population of salmon thriving in its waters. It provides a good research model for other relatively unspoiled habitats. In 2003 the smolt wheel was just beginning to prove itself as a reliable record for trapping and counting the juveniles (smolts) during their downstream migration. We found out that the young smolts generally remain in the river for three years before they take their first trip into the ocean. The majority of these leaves the river at the onset of low tide and swims an average of forty-four days to leave the Gulf of St. Lawrence for the wider ocean.

Much later, they return as adults to the riverside. These salmon are angled on a fly rod and released into a holding cage positioned in the water near the shore. The following day, the fish are fitted with an acoustic tag. The acoustic transmitters are implanted into the abdominal cavity of smolts and adult salmon. There are small ones for the smolts and larger ones for the adult salmon. Recovery after surgery takes about six hours, and the salmon are then released to

resume their spawning migration. To date, transmitters have been surgically inserted in 215 salmon smolts, and 59 in adult salmon. The adult transmitters have a life of two years while the juveniles' smaller transmitters stay activated for two months.

There are receivers arranged along the river's edge by Dr. Whoriskey. He suits up in a wet suit and an oxygen tank and places them early in June. The receivers are set to record the date and time of passage of any tagged fish that swims within five hundred metres (547 yards). Usually, the receivers are recovered in August and the information is then downloaded into the main database. A few receivers are deployed again in the river at that time to record adult salmon movements in the river in the fall, winter, and early spring. Receivers have also been positioned in different locations around the Gulf of St. Lawrence and into the wider ocean area along the Strait of Belle Isle and Cabot Strait (the southern exit to the Atlantic Ocean from the Gulf of St. Lawrence, located between Newfoundland and Cape Breton, Nova Scotia).

Over the years of research, the tagged salmon helped us unravel wonderful details of their journey in the river and in the ocean. One of the main findings in the river was the discovery that most of the tagged fish overwinter in the river after spawning and await the following spring to leave the river and the gulf as kelts (black salmon).

Once they leave the river, salmon are more difficult to track, but the receiver array spanning the width of the Strait of Belle Isle detected a few of the tagged adults. In 2007, for the first time, two tagged adult salmon from the Rivière St-Jean were detected at the Strait of Belle Isle. They had both been both caught the year before in Deforest Pool, one by James J. Hill III (James J. Hill's great-grandson) on June 9, 2006 (818 mm / 32 in) and one by Mari Hill Harpur, Jim's cousin and James J. Hill's great-granddaughter (838 mm / 33 in) on June 15, 2006. These salmon had overwintered in the river in 2006 and left the gulf the following year, 2007. Mari's salmon arrived

Surgery at Riverside, 2010

Top to bottom

Yvon Beaudin (left) and Gilles Maloney fetch the salmon in preparation for surgery.

Left to right: Guide Gilles Maloney; Luisa C. Miller from Chicago, Illinois; Scott Petty from San Antonio, Texas; guide Louis Earnest Dérosby; and Marylise Lefèvre prepare the fish for surgery. This fish would be caught in Greenland some fifteen months later.

Marylise inserts the transmitter into the fish's stomach cavity.

Marylise Lefèvre, Luisa Miller, Louis Ernest Dérosby, photographed by Dr. Bradley Thurston in 2010 with the fish that provided us a great migration clue.

PHOTOS: MARI HILL HARPUR – MHH PERSONAL COLLECTION

first at the strait in late June 2007, and Jim's salmon followed a month later. Of the two, Jim's fish left the river after we deployed the receiver and was detected leaving the river on June 17, 2007; as a result we were able to calculate the time of travel to the northern exit of the Gulf of St. Lawrence: thirty-seven days to travel approximately 650 kilometres (404 miles).

Ironically, on June 21, 2007, Jim Hill fished another salmon with his guide Jocelyn Beaudin (775 mm / 30.5 in). That fish jumped 30 Mile Falls at the end of July of that year only to come back downriver after spawning at the end of October. But the fish stayed in the river until the following year when he was detected crossing the Strait of Belle Isle early in July 2008.

In the following years, we made sure to have some receivers in place close to the estuary early in the spring to witness the salmon's time of departure. The fastest salmon to reach the Strait of Belle Isle after leaving the river as a kelt took only eighteen days! It was caught by Thomas Knight (Anson Beard's party) and his guide Yoland Beaudin (800 mm / 31.5 in) on June 16, 2008.

In 2009 Dr. Jim King, a guest from Hamilton, Bermuda, tagged a salmon that gave us yet another piece of the migration puzzle. Jim and his guide, Robin Chambers (great-grandson of Benjamin Chambers Sr.) caught a 787-millimetre (31-inch) salmon that was tagged and released the following day. The following spring that fish was detected swimming by one of the receivers deployed along the western point of Anticosti Island, six days after leaving the Rivière Saint-Jean. Forty days later it was detected swimming through the Strait of Belle Isle. This was the first evidence that salmon do not necessarily choose the shortest route out of the gulf (a 650 kilometre / 404 mile trip) but instead may travel around Anticosti Island on an eight-hundred-kilometre (five-hundred-mile) journey.

Finally, one of the fish caught by a Hill Camp guest, Luisa Miller, and her guide, Louis Ernest Dérosby, gave us one of the greatest migration clues of our salmon's journey. On June 22, 2010, Luisa caught a 787 mm (31 in) spawner that we tagged and released (tag code 57948). Thanks to a scale sample taken at that time, that salmon was judged to be five years old: three years spent in the river as a juvenile and two years of growth in the ocean before it returned to the river to spawn for the first time. Caught in its spawning migration and released June 23, 2010, in Rivière St-Jean, weighing 5.4 kg (12 lbs, Pesola scale). It overwintered in the river and was detected on July 9, 2011, crossing the Strait of Belle Isle. He was fished seventy-four days later (on September 22, 2011) off Greenland (south of Nuuk) by a fisherman using a gillnet. The fish was sampled and the tag was no longer functioning. However, it was sent to VEMCO and they were able to retrieve the tag's ID. The fish was received gutted (gutted weight: 6.16 kg / 13.5 lb) and was measured to be 850 mm (33.5 in) fork length. Too bad for that fish, but it gave us precious information.

Dr. Jim King and David Lines from Bermuda.
PHOTO: MARI HILL HARPUR, JULY 2009 – MHH PERSONAL COLLECTION

Yesterday, Today, Tomorrow

Each individual river has its own biodiversity fuelled by the specific genetics of the animals adapted to their particular environment. The St. John is host to salmon whose average three-winter weight is between 4.5 and 5.4 kg (10 and 12 lbs). Their eggs are laid in various spawning beds along the river system. The salmon will spend up to four summers and winters in this river before they migrate as smolts into the northern Atlantic along the waters of western Greenland. The lucky and hardy ones live long enough to make a trip through the wide Atlantic Ocean to their traditional feeding grounds at least two or three times.

The salmon move in both the river and the sea to the rhythm of the seasons. Smolts that move out to sea head for Greenland where they remain, feeding during that first summer, and stay somewhere in the North Atlantic ocean through winter before perhaps returning to Greenland for another summer and then turning for home. Meanwhile, in fresh water, in the early months of the New Year, as the ice starts to break up, the adults that have spent the winter in the river start to move south back to the ocean. Those that take their time and move out late will cross paths with the newly arriving spawners that are beginning to return to the St. John River. These fish will have travelled the northern Atlantic for one to three visits through the wide-open sea before returning to their rivers of birth. The fish migrations between spawning may last for one to three "sea winters." They will always return to the same river system to spawn. This event takes place yearly in hundreds of rivers, from Spain to Russia in Europe, and Maine to Labrador and Northern Quebec in North America. Providing protection for this annual migration is the responsibility of governments and private individuals alike. Without everyone's continued participation and the use of correct tools, all ocean traffic—fish, mammals, or human industry—is impacted. It is our inherent duty to protect and nurture the salmon's environment, as well as our own.

∞

There is a lot to think about when you live on the side of a river. Sitting in those rocking chairs at Hill Camp, the same ones that have been there since the beginning, I watch the canopy of stars rising behind the moon as I look southeast. The stories of friends embellish the evening sky, and the night creatures sing in a wild harmony.

Four small salmon were caught this afternoon, with flies so tiny you can hardly see the eye to knot it on the leader. The pleasure of the river washing below our canoe still feels real.

Tonight the river guards shine their light while their dog runs along the shore. They follow the scents of forest animals: moose, bears, wolves. They smell for the poachers. Cooking fires slowly diminish and bats fly around the buildings. Everyone has gathered to see and hear the returning salmon. There is a sense of celebration in the air.

In the morning, I like to wake up early. I wait until I hear Jocelyn (Tintin) Beaudin set the house fire at around 5:30 a.m. I know it is time. I go and sit on the porch and watch the river fog lift and burn off as the sun rises. The water is so still and black it seems to stop flowing. The wind that searches for our fly lines during the late morning has not begun. The world is quiet and the smell of the wood fire permeates the camp. As the morning mist rises, something catch my eye. It looks as if someone is walking down the steps to the beach. The vision makes an odd impression. It looks like a man. I do not recognize him. But I think I hear him say:

All is at the ready, Sir.
Welcome back,
Salmo salar,
to your home.

I shake my head and look again at the vague form vanishing at the river's edge. I think I see John Justin Toomey standing by the water's edge with his hand outstretched. His is a warm and welcoming gesture. Then, I see the figure slowly disappear, and I wonder.

Left to right: Dave Wilson of Toronto, Ontario; Robert Vanier of Montreal; and Dr. Altaf Kassam of Toronto are dressed in turn-of-the-century fashion.

Dr. Gabrielle Slowey and Sara Maud in period clothing.

The Last Cast

*"A game fish is too valuable
to be caught only once."*

—Lee Wulff, 1939

Lee Wulff, a renowned sportsman, author, fly tier, and enthusiastic outdoorsman, coined this phrase over seventy years ago, drawing attention to the dwindling recreational fishing stocks on the Eastern Seaboard. Wulff was particularly passionate about the Atlantic salmon. During his long career, he succeeded in transforming the intentions of the sport-fishing industry, while working diligently to establish a category for fish protection called "Game Fish Status." That approach would pave the way for today's catch-and-release practice.

The shadows of the past have caught up with us. On the side of the river we see the past and the present. It is within our grasp. Our combined experiences bode well for the future of the returning salmon. Our research has indicated that the river is a healthy habitat for the species. There are some predators, but it is a manageable situation if security and diligence are professionally applied, and if our conscience is allowed to guide us. The St. John River is healthy, and with no plans for industrial intervention we should look forward to nurturing a healthy salmon population for many years to come.

The wide-open oceans, where problems are being addressed and monitored, are another matter. One of the more promising research facilities, directed by Dr. Fred Whoriskey, is the Ocean Tracking Network (OTN) based at Dalhousie University in Halifax, Nova Scotia. Through the continued emphasis on acoustic tracking, individual assistance from groups like Hill Camp, and considerable governmental support, our success extends beyond the national forum into the international arena. The continued participation of individual anglers from all regions is paramount. Individually, we need the ability to understand and maintain the health and safety of Earth's marine environment. It is important to provide good management at the riverbank and then let that knowledge flow around the world's five oceans.

It was once thought that a caught fish was a dead fish, but thanks to sports like Mr. Wulff and many others, the world of catch and release would evolve and become accepted practice. A detailed description of catch and release was borrowed from my cousin Anson M. Beard Jr.'s privately published book, *A Life in Full Sail*:

> *Standing in the canoe, at the river's edge there was a flash of silver. We brought her into the net. The hook fell out of her mouth as we lifted her into the fresh river water in the panier, a basket specifically designed for Hill Camp. The fish rested lightly in the canoe while we took a quick scale sample and its length measurement. We rocked her in the current to resuscitate her oxygen flow, released her and she swam away to spawn her eggs and be caught another day.*

In 2012 I took this 81.3-centimetre (32-inch) fish and successfully released her seconds after the photograph was taken.
Photo: Louis Ernest Derosby – MHH Personal Collection

Image and size comparison of the barbless Silver Doctor #8 fly that caught the fish in the above photo.
Photo: Mari Hill Harpur, 2012 – MHH Personal Collection

Guide Robin Chambers taking the last cast of the day with
Jill Edgett from Moncton, New Brunswick, 2007.

Max (Robert) Vanier with his father Robert Vanier and guide Gilles Maloney, getting ready to release a large fish.

The Honourable Bob (Robert) Smith discussing his afternoon's fishing experience with Max (Robert) Vanier and Doug Harpur.

When Lefty Kreh, the legendary eighty-six-year-old doyen of fly casting, was interviewed in 2013 by an Australian writer for *Fly Life: Australia and New Zealand*, Lefty commented on the state of North American fishing rivers:

> *The time is fast approaching in the US when to have good fishing you almost need to have it on private land. The public does not take care of public water very well; they trash it and they over-poach it. I know that goes against the face of what everyone wants to hear, but the truth of the matter is that when you let people run amok to let them do what they want, a certain percentage of those people are going to make it very disruptive, and it ends up the property will be closed to the public.*

Lefty puts the root of this problem squarely on the lack of discipline at home and in schools, saying that once you lose discipline in younger people you've lost everything.

> *It's almost like dominoes being tripped over and it starts with the discipline in the kids. To me it is so damn simple and most people can't see it. Parents don't take their children outdoors to do things anymore, so the children gravitate to electronic devices and they have lost complete appreciation for the outdoors.*
>
> *When we were younger we walked places, rode bikes, and went hunting and fishing, and your parents and your uncles took you fishing.*

Jocelyn (Tintin) Beaudin cleaning out the canoe in the evening.
PHOTO: MARI HILL HARPUR, 2005 – MHH PERSONAL COLLECTION

Appendix I

Biographies

	Louis W. Jr. – Elsi Hill	Mari Hill Harpur
Louis W. Sr.	Cortlandt	James J. Hill III
Charlotte	Norman Slade*	
James J. Hill	Ruth	Anson Beard Sr.
Rachel	Gertrude (Tudie) Boeckmann ffolliott	
Gertrude		

* Richard Slade gave his "votes" to Anson Sr.

Note: After re-organization in 1988, ownership fell to Mari Hill Harpur, James J. Hill III, Elsi Hill, Louis W. Hill Jr.

James J. Hill (1838 – 1916)

On September 16, 1838, James Jerome Hill was born in the farming village of Rockwood, Upper Canada (Ontario). As a boy he attended Rockwood Academy and received training in math and science. He worked at the general store in the village, where he learned the basic concepts of accounting. After the death of his father, when James was seventeen years old, he set out on foot with his savings of six hundred dollars. In Toronto he procured passage on a boat that would take him "somewhere else, anywhere else." He eventually arrived at the Mississippi River in a small town called Pig's Eye, Minnesota (later to be named St. Paul). He worked in a steamboat transfer firm until he was twenty-eight, when he struck out on his own to establish James J. Hill and Company, a transportation and warehouse business. A year later he married Mary Theresa Mehegan from New York City. It was to be a lucky and happy marriage. They had ten children, and Mary proved to be every bit as much an organizer as her husband. Together they built a considerable empire.

Between 1877 and 1879, Hill acquired the St. Paul & Pacific Railway with Norman Kittson, Donald Smith, George Stephen, and John Kennedy. Hill renamed the company St. Paul, Minneapolis & Manitoba Railroad, and served as its general manager. Three years later he became president. In 1880, some twenty years after he had established himself in Minnesota, he became a United States citizen. Hill continued to have several important business relationships in Canada, and he played an early role in the construction of the Canadian Pacific Railway. Ten years later, in 1890, Hill renamed his company the Great Northern Railway. By 1893 the Great Northern track ran from the western

James J. Hill's grandson Louis W. Hill Jr. stands by the side of Hill's canoe in 1912. Young Louis was to visit Hill Camp in 1912, 1914, and 1915. After those visits with his grandfather and father, he later returned as a married man with his wife Elsi Hill, family, and other friends from the 1960s to the 1980s.
PHOTO: LOUIS W. HILL SR. – MHH PERSONAL COLLECTION

border of Minnesota to Seattle, Washington, all paid for with private funding. There was not a drop of government money involved. He had finally reached his goal: the Pacific Ocean. From that initial sum of six hundred dollars he had saved as a seventeen-year-old boy, he had created an empire worth more than $50 million. This was quite an achievement for a man, as cousin Dick Slade recounts, "whose only motto was hard work."

Louis W. Hill Sr. (1872–1948)

Research shows that all James J. Hill's children—especially Clara, Charlotte, and of course Louis—made extensive use of cameras during their lifetimes. At first, they took photographs with the Kodak box camera invented by George Eastman in 1888. That year, at age sixteen, Louis was attending Phillips Exeter Academy in New Hampshire, USA, when he wrote of sending home photos of his room on campus. That first-edition camera was a wooden box, a simple lens, and a shutter. It cost $22.00. The cost included the film (already installed in the camera), which had one hundred exposures. After exposing the film, one mailed the entire camera back to the Eastman Company. The film was processed, prints were made, and the camera was refilled with film and returned to the owner. By 1889 the camera's delicate paper film had been replaced by a more resilient, plastic-based film. As an enterprising amateur, Louis could learn to handle his own processing and his little Kodak would become his regular companion. He was obviously fascinated by and proficient in the "new science" of photography.

During his life, Louis was never far behind the latest in emerging film technology. He consistently upgraded his equipment, purchasing new and improved cameras. In 1916 he purchased a Folding Pocket Brownie Vest Pocket Kodak, and in 1918, a Kodak Junior. These cameras were easy to handle and convenient to carry with him at all times. He never gave up his love of the light box, and by the end of his life, he had produced a respectable collection of photographs—evident by the more than six thousand photographs catalogued in his private papers. And those were only the images he chose to have printed!

∞

Louis, my grandfather, was the third child of James J. and Mary Hill. Like his siblings, he was born in St. Paul, Minnesota. He received his college degree from Yale University in 1893. In 1901 Louis married Maud Van Cortlandt Taylor in New York City. The couple had four children: Louis Jr., Maud, Jerome, and Cortlandt. As their children were born, Louis' photographic pursuits accelerated. His children's lives are well documented. He recorded family activities and trips and also took his camera along on the fishing excursions to the St. John River with his father. He took hundreds of photographs while on the river, many of which he shared with his father's fishing companions. For example, in 1914 Louis wrote John Toomey: "Herewith two enlarged photographs of Mr. Hannaford on the River. Will you please hold these to be sent up to the River to add to the collection there? I shall furnish Mr. Hannaford some extra copies." Louis made eleven trips to the St. John with his father and often brought his camera and sketchbook along. Many of these photographs and sketches are the source of the early images of Hill Camp.

Shortly after his graduation from university, Louis went to work with his father at the Great Northern Railway. He served in many departments of the company, and in 1907 succeeded James J. Hill as president. In 1912 he was named chairman of the board, and, after

Louis W. Hill Sr., with three large fish held on a pole by a guide. Since Louis Sr. took most of Hill Camp's early photographs, he was rarely represented as a subject.

Photo: Unknown – Hill Family Collection – Minnesota Historical Society

Louis W. Hill Sr. was an artist and photographer. He painted this oil painting of the scenery at 30 Mile Falls.
PHOTO: MHH PERSONAL COLLECTION

his father's death in 1916, Louis became the leader and face of the Hill railroad lines.

Louis shared many of his father's characteristics when it came to running the railway empire James J. Hill had built. He had a smart business sense, possessing both a wide view of possibilities and a very precise attention to detail. Having the luxury of second-generation wealth, Louis gave support to several entities during his lifetime. Although he was a very hard worker, he also took time to enjoy life in the outdoors. He brought his eldest son, Louis W. Hill Jr., to the river in 1912 when the boy was ten years old.

In addition to Louis and his younger brother Walter, the family members who are listed in the record book as having made just one trip to the river with James J. Hill include Hill's oldest son, James Norman, and sons-in-law Anson Beard, George Slade, and Egil Boeckmann.

The upper reaches of the leased property, close to 30 Mile Falls where the Deforest house once stood. Louis W. Hill Sr. loved the outdoors and hunting and fishing. Louis Sr. made eleven trips to the St. John River with his father and always brought a camera along.
PHOTO: LOUIS W. HILL SR. – MINNESOTA HISTORICAL SOCIETY

James J. Hill's Descendants and the Progression of Hill Camp Ownership

When Hill died intestate in 1916, the salmon river ownership was divided equally among the Hill family members. His five children, Louis, Charlotte, Ruth, Rachel, and Gertrude, purchased the river's shares from the estate and became equal owners of the river. In 1916, the appraised value of the St. John property, including personal property at the site, was agreed upon as $25,000.

In 1919, three years after Hill's death, his sons–in–law George Slade (Charlotte's husband) and Anson Beard (Ruth's husband) brought a party to the river. In September 1919, Slade drew up a proposed agreement for the management of the river, which dealt with issues of leases, costs, possible sale of individual shares, administration, and other issues including who, where, and how many should be allowed to fish in a season.

Sara Maud Vanier with son Max (Robert) Vanier, James J. Hill's great-great-great grandson in 2011.

Family guests at the turn of the new century

Clockwise from top left:

Jim Hill (James J. Hill III), great-grandson of James J. Hill, standing above 30 Mile Falls.

Jim Hill, this time holding a grilse.

Sara and Doug with salmon, 2001.

Doug Harpur and Ann ffolliott; Gertrude Gavin's niece, 2003.

Me, Doug, Sara Maud, James J. Hill III, and Cody (James J. Hill IV) in Longue-Pointe-de-Mingan, 2001.

Mrs. Tracy Hill.

Jim Hill (James J. Hill III), Tracy, and Sheena Hill, in 1985.

PHOTOS: MARI HILL HARPUR — MHH PERSONAL COLLECTION

The Chambers Family and a North Shore Tale

The North Shore and Labrador is a world unto itself. Due to the hazardous living conditions, extreme distances between settlements, and relatively small populations, everyone in this remote area knows and helps one another. Settlements can be isolated for much of the year, so kindness is a feature of communal values. As generations evolved in this area, so did the culture of charity that characterized the villagers' many extended relationships. The settlement along the St. John River has been no different. Its inhabitants, too, have traditionally practiced generosity and kindness.

By 1923 James J. Hill had been dead seven years, and the use of the river property was divided between Hill's children and grandchildren. At this point the management of the river, which had so long been the domain of the Chambers family, passed to the third manager, Charles Maloney Jr. (1887 – 1958), who was married to Benjamin Chambers Sr.'s ninth child, Marie-Anne (Mary). Young Charles's father, Charles Maloney Sr., had come from York, England, in the late 1800s and settled in the Gaspésie, Quebec. After a few years, he sailed with his family to Mingan, the neighbouring village to St-Jean. In this way, the Maloney family was similar to that of Benjamin Chambers Sr., who had also travelled the Atlantic to the North Shore by boat from the Gaspésie. As well, the Chambers and Maloney families are related. Jean Chambers, the current Hill Camp manager, is married to Sylvie Maloney. Sylvie's family also showed a leadership that is typical of the local values. Sylvie's great-aunt, the great-granddaughter of Charles Maloney Sr., was Maud Watt. Maud was referred to as "the Angel of the North" in a book about her life by William Ashley Anderson. Clearly, Maud, the sister of Charles Maloney Jr., represents those qualities of our northern culture that are most remarkable.

Maud Watt was the first conservation officer in Canada. Her husband, Jim Watt, started working for the Hudson's Bay Company in 1915. In 1919 he became the factor of Rupert House, an extremely remote outpost on Hudson Bay. It was not long before he and Maud were contributing to their small community. They were captivated by their new friends and the indigenous culture. However, the Watts were also quite concerned with the living conditions in the area around Hudson Bay. They began to realize that the Native population had little food. People were starving to death. Word

Above: John Chambers.
PHOTO: LOUIS W. HILL SR., 1915 – MINNESOTA HISTORICAL SOCIETY

At right, top to bottom: Mari Hill Harpur and Jean Chambers with salmon prepared to release after its surgery.
PHOTO: UNKNOWN, 2010 – MHH PERSONAL COLLECTION

Harold Chambers stands behind the replica of the Hill Camp house that he built during the winter of 1995 – 1996 after studying the original architecture plans. Harold was born January 19, 1923, and died in November 2001. He managed the camp for Mrs. Gavin, Louis, and Corty Hill. During this time, Harold also operated his own store in the village of St-Jean.
PHOTO: MARI HILL HARPUR, 1996 – MHH PERSONAL COLLECTION

Jean (left) and Harold Chambers (right) with their afternoon catch.
PHOTO: MARI HILL HARPUR, 1996 – MHH PERSONAL COLLECTION

Jean Chambers waves goodbye from the beach at Hill Camp.
PHOTO: MARI HILL HARPUR, 2008 – MHH PERSONAL COLLECTION

The Chambers Connection to Hill Camp

1st manager   Benjamin Chambers Sr. (1900 – 1902).

2nd manager   Robert (Sonny) Chambers (1900 – 1915), Benjamin's first son. Sonny and Benjamin Sr. jointly managed Hill Camp.

3rd manager   Esther Wright (Sonny's wife) and her son Wenceslas (Wallace) Chambers (1916 – 1922) jointly managed Hill Camp.

4th manager   Charles Maloney Jr. (1923 – 1956) was married to Marie-Anne (Mary) Chambers (ninth child of Benjamin Sr.). Charles Jr. had two siblings, Maud and Georges. Charlie managed Hill Camp for Gertrude Gavin.

5th manager   Harold Chambers (1957 – 1988), Benjamin Chambers Jr.'s son and Benjamin Chambers Sr.'s grandson.

6th manager   Jean Chambers (1989 – present), Harold Chambers' son, Benjamin Chambers Sr.'s great-grandson.

would come to Rupert House of small encampments where all the families had perished. To make things worse, because of the disruption of the war in 1917, the annual supply ship that brought food and provisions had been designated for other work and had not been able to bring the necessary supplies to the north.

The Watts knew they had to help their neighbours. By 1929 events had become even more tragic. The beaver, which in the area had traditionally provided food and livelihood for the Natives, had been overhunted to near-extinction. Something had to be done. Maud came up with a plan to reintroduce the beaver into the local ecosystem. She pulled strings that made her officially the Warden of Rupert House—not an easy task for a woman in those days. And so, on her own, Maud set about to create and administer the Rupert House Preserve, an area of 484,587 square kilometres (187,000 square miles). Maud needed to travel from Rupert House to Sept-Îles to negotiate the pending deal. As a result, she was the first white woman to walk and canoe from Fort Chimo (Kuujjuaq) through Ungava Bay, following the Moisie River to arrive in Sept-Îles.

Hauling their supplies by hand, Maud and her husband, their two children (aged three and six), and a Native family walked fifty-five days to travel the approximately 1,827 kilometres (800 miles) from Rupert House to Sept-Îles. In less than two cold winter months (April 9 – June 2, 1918), they arrived at their destination, and there they finalized the document that created the Rupert House Preserve. After the preserve was in place, she and the indigenous peoples in the area successfully reintroduced the beaver. Maud and her husband effectively prevented many deaths and illnesses among the regional population.

As a result of her efforts, Maud was honoured with the rank of Cree chieftain. She wrote the first dictionary of the local people's language and subsequently translated that into Montagnais, French, and English. Hers is a story of amazing resilience and fortitude.

The Maloneys, like the Chambers family, spoke English in their early days. However, also like the Chambers, after three generations they had adopted French as their primary language.

Charles Maloney Jr., served as the river guardian for James J. Hill's heirs until 1957. From 1957 to 1988, Harold Chambers (1923 – 2001), Benjamin Chambers Sr.'s grandson, managed Hill Camp for Hill family members who were actively involved at the camp. The Chambers family continues to play an important part in the river's management. In 1989 Harold's son, Jean Chambers, took over management of the camp and continues in that position today.

The original families who lived in the village of Rivière-St-Jean in the late 1800s were the Chambers, Maloney, Wright, Parisee, Beaudin, Dérosby, Edwards, Léveque, Girard, Chapados, Paguet, and Leblanc families. Of those families, the Chambers, Maloneys and Wrights have worked side by side through the generations at Hill Camp.

This traditional Montagnais tea doll was made in 2012 in Labrador by Theresa Andrews, from Northwest River, in the village of Sheshatshui. The Montagnais are a traditionally nomadic Innu people. Everyone, including the children, helped to support and carry loads during their annual migration from summer to winter camps. Tea dolls like this one played a dual role of suitcase and toy—it would have been stuffed with Labrador tea at the beginning of the migration, and as the journey progressed the tea would be removed and brewed to sustain the travellers. Moss would have been used to fill the empty cavity until the family returned to the summer hunting grounds, where more tea would be gathered and stored in the doll. The face and the mittens of the mother and child are made from caribou skin (although some dolls like this were made of seal skin). If you place your nose close to the doll, you can still smell the tea. Labrador tea is a bush tea native to the North Shore and Labrador. Raw leaves are poisonous, but tea made from the boiled leaves is said to be fortifying.

PHOTO: MARI HILL HARPUR – MHH PERSONAL COLLECTION

Labrador tea (*Ledum latifolium Rhododendron groenlandicum*), drawn by William Miller, from The Botanical Cabinet. London: John & Arthur Arch, 1818. Plate 534.

Robert C. Minor (1868 – 1947)

Robert (Bob) Minor, born in Louisiana, moved to St. Paul, Minnesota, in the 1890s. He began working as a porter for the railroad in 1893, and in 1896 he transferred to James J. Hill's private car as head porter. He handled procurement of supplies and did the cooking both on the car and at the St. John River. He made sure things always ran smoothly, whether he was arranging for business trips or delivering a birthday cake to Charlotte Hill. Minor had a desk outside Hill's office in the Great Northern building in St. Paul. He travelled with Hill on his business trips, fishing vacations in Quebec, and with various family members. Minor took good care of Hill and was a trusted employee. He attended all the fishing trips to the St. John with Hill, and Bob's son, Walter, joined him on several occasions. Incidentally, Walter went on to earn a medical degree at the University of Minnesota. After Hill's death, Mary Hill chose Bob to be one of the honorary pallbearers at her husband's funeral.

Bob died at his daughter's home in Asheville, North Carolina, on May 12, 1947. The Great Northern Railway arranged for his body to be returned to St. Paul for the funeral. When he died, Louis Hill Jr., wrote a letter to Minor's son, Walter: "He was a dear friend and I do not think that I have many friends who I have known as long."

Robert (Bob) Minor with son Walter at Hill Camp.
Photo: Louis W. Hill Sr., 1901 – MHH Personal Collection

Photo: Unknown – Minnesota Historical Society

John Justin Toomey (1858 – 1942)

John Justin Toomey served the Hill family for almost half a century. Born in Canada, Toomey was in his thirteenth year with the Grand Trunk Railway in Montreal when he was recruited in 1888 to come to St. Paul, Minnesota, to work for James J. Hill. At that time, his brother, William, was Hill's private secretary. The Toomey brothers became Hill's head bookkeepers, the only ones who dealt with their employer's personal accounts. William Toomey left Hill's employ in 1904, and John stepped into his brother's shoes.

When the search for a salmon river in Quebec began, John was the logical person to be Hill's man on the ground in Montreal because he had many connections from his time living in that city. He quickly became Hill's eyes and ears, and hands and feet, for all the negotiations that led to the acquisition of the St. John River property. Toomey was also instrumental in the construction projects on the river property, and he worked closely over the years with the Chambers family. Toomey made the arrangements for the fishing trips and accompanied Hill to the river to ensure the visits went smoothly. Nothing escaped Toomey's notice, and nothing was considered insignificant, no matter how minute the issue. His talents were numerous and varied. He negotiated with the Quebec government on lease arrangements even as he pointed out inventory details to the Chambers family.

After the death of James J. Hill, Toomey continued to work for the family. He handled Mary Hill's business and personal affairs until her death in 1921. He assisted Louis Sr. with the administration of the Hill estate. Toomey also served on the boards of a number of Hill family business concerns.

Always a man of intensity and detail, John Toomey wrote the following description of the St. John River after an early visit in May 1900:

There is a harbor for vessels drawing six-feet of water, or less. The navigation of the river, above the first five-six miles where the tide ends, is accomplished with canoes. Due to rapids and currents, for much of this distance upstream the canoes must be poled. There are only a few stretches of the river where paddles can be used.

Fishing from canoes is the best option as there is little opportunity to fish from the shore, although many pools could be fished by wading in.

John J. Toomey died at the age of eighty-four on January 27, 1942.

Biologists, Guides, and Residents: Streamside Research and Beyond

The following biology students have been active in administrating the research program at Hill Camp:

1998	**Susanne Mills**, research assistant
1999	**Jean Carreau**, research assistant
2000	**Andy Moss**, research assistant
2001–2005	**Gino Doucette**, biologist, Atlantic Salmon Federation
2006–2011	**Marylise Lefèvre**, research assistant and MSc Candidate
2012	**Kim Whoriskey**, research assistant

The following local guides and residents were also instrumental in advancing our research program. They were active in helping in various activities, from detailed surgery to healthy streamside resuscitation. Additionally, they responded to many requests for canoe transport along the river and general management of the camp. All of these individuals made a significant contribution. Without them there would have been little hope of the success of our program.

Jocelyn Beaudin

Yvon Beaudin

Yoland Beaudin

Jean Chambers

Robin Chambers

Louis-Ernest Dérosby

Gilles Maloney

Far left: James J. Hill III, Doug Harpur, and Kim Whoriskey.
PHOTO: MARI HILL HARPUR, 2001 – MHH PERSONAL COLLECTION

Left: Kim Whoriskey, research assistant, eleven years later in front of the canoes at Hill Camp.
PHOTO: MARI HILL HARPUR, 2012 – MHH PERSONAL COLLECTION

Appendix II
Fish Tales: Friendships and Frivolity

So many remarkable happenings occur at a fishing camp. Often, people bring their personal gifts to the river. While Doug and I were busy reorganizing the camp's structure, we did not anticipate the excitement and satisfaction that accompanied our increased involvement with Hill Camp's visitors and guests. We enjoyed them and appreciated the interesting things that made their Hill Camp visit special. We delighted in their interactions with the guides and the camp's support crew, as well as with one another and ourselves. In countless ways, the wonderful and curious guests who have participated in the modern Hill Camp experience have enhanced our own angling experience. While we were fortunate in knowing many people who fished, we found our own fishing skills improved by our interactions with the guests. It was not so much learning what their secrets were but observing how they would apply their skills to the task at hand. Every season we looked forward to the camaraderie, the storytelling, and the friendships that sparked amongst this eclectic group of peers. The camp continued to be a place where many different people gathered to enjoy a relaxed camaraderie while sampling the bounty of the St. John River. Following are some of the anecdotes that I have overheard and collected while staying at camp over the many years.

∞

My cousin, Anson McCook Beard Jr., from New York City, returned to Hill Camp as our guest in 1994. He has been a regular angler since his first visit to Hill Camp when he was fifteen years old. Anson has inherited his father's attention to detail and a desire to practice conservation ethics in his personal surroundings. Throughout his life, Anson has visited and fished on a global scale but the St. John River always holds a particularly affectionate place in his heart. One of his early comments to us about our management of the camp was that it "ran like a Swiss clock." I must

The flags flying at the top of the camp stairs are a welcoming sight after a long journey to camp.
PHOTO: MARI HILL HARPUR, 2013 – MHH PERSONAL COLLECTION

say I had not thought of the camp in that way, but I knew what he meant. Doug and I have managed to pull together all sorts of divergent characteristics of our fishing camp so that they interact appropriately. Five years later, when Anson returned to Hill Camp, one of his guests caught a salmon that would turn out to be a shining star in our angler-sponsored research program. That was a very proud moment for all of us. For Anson, fishing and business seemed to go together. He has been through a lot of rapids, both physical and conceptual. As a former managing director and inside board member of Morgan Stanley, he was part of the group that took Apple Computer public. Perhaps relying on strategy and collaboration is the secret to the success of his lucrative undertakings. His favourite fly? In the 1950s and 1960s on the St. John River his go-to fishing fly was a Nighthawk (silver body, black dressing). Now, that is a fly any salmon would be hard-pressed to ignore!

∞

When Norb Berg, from Barronnet, Wisconsin, was at camp, it rocked with laughter. Norb began working with Control Data Corporation when the company went from 180 employees to 57,000. His career in many ways brought new meaning to the function of corporate human relations and social responsibility. As a psychologist he had an uncanny ability to sense the lighter side of

Norb Berg at Hill Camp with his catch.
PHOTO: MARI HILL HARPUR — MHH PERSONAL COLLECTION

issues. One story he shared was about Seymour Cray, with whom he worked. Cray had developed a series of machines that were the fastest computers in the world. Typically, Cray enjoyed working alone but when the president of the company, William Norris, needed to have Cray's five-year projected work plan approved by the board, Norb's expertise was desperately solicited. Days passed and finally Norb went into Cray's office and begged him for his report. The next morning Norb found the report waiting for him on his desk. It was two sentences long: "Fifth year: make the world's fastest computer. First year: one fifth of the above." Norb's favourite words of river wisdom are: "Love many and trust few, but always paddle your own canoe." I recall one day that he was serious. He turned to me and said, "What is said in camp stays in camp!"

∞

Jake Eberts, the filmmaker and director, was filming Robert Redford's movie *A River Runs Through It* when he fished at our camp in 1992. When he told me he never used a real fish in the entire movie, I thought that was odd. I could not imagine that robot

Right, top: Jacques Giroux cradling his first salmon.
PHOTO: MARI HILL HARPUR, 2011 — MHH PERSONAL COLLECTION

Right: Jacques with his son-in-law Jordan Harpur.
PHOTOS: MARI HILL HARPUR — MHH PERSONAL COLLECTION,

fish would really portray an interesting image, let alone contribute to an engaging story. It would not be until I had seen the movie twice that I remembered this anecdote. View any of Jake's films and, as an onlooker you will no longer feel like an observer. Instead, you will have the sensation of being a bona fide participant. You will feel as if you are part of the action. What a gift Jake possessed. No wonder his various films won a staggering thirty-seven Oscars.

∞

Jacques Giroux from Montreal, Quebec retired from teaching several years ago. Since then, Jacques has had time to hunt and fish. He discovered that fishing for salmon is challenging. He had fished for five years for the elusive king of sport fish before he came to

Hill Camp. There, on his first day of fishing, he took a fish. The joy he felt was palpable, and in celebration he wrote and composed a beautiful song called "Ode to Hill Camp." Jacques's family comes from a long line of ancient and modern troubadours. He surprised us by playing his guitar and singing the song he had written to celebrate his first Atlantic salmon. This is his beautiful song, which he accompanies on his guitar.

> All along the river
> On my way to Hill Camp
> Dazzled by wits of the past
> My mind drifted quite fast.
>
> I could see pioneers ghosting up the river
> I could hear their whispers of satisfaction
> I could feel their breathless expression
> Like me overrun and bewitched by that nature.
>
> Full of idle fancy, I tasted that moment
> Like in a fairy tale I bow to the king.
> Time of a flash in the pan, I felt like a giant,
> It's hard to believe but it wasn't a dream.
>
> As night, suddenly, wafted in its darkness,
> Embraced by the shadow's and silence's fullness
> Cuddled against each other and bound by memories
> Cabin logs remember themselves a century.
>
> I've been to Hill Camp
> I've been to paradise
> It will forever remain in my mind.
> It will forever remain
> Etched in my heart,
> Etched in my heart.

∞

John Hampton said simply, "I want to go on at least one productive fishing trip every year for the rest of my life." And he did. We were fortunate to fish with John at Hill Camp, as well as other places. He was an unassuming and true sport when it came to fly-fishing. He

John Hampton choosing his fly and writing his diary.

Left to right: Donald Thom, Alan Macdougall and Doug Harpur.

PHOTO: MARI HILL HARPUR, 2013 – MHH PERSONAL COLLECTION

Doug Harpur and Gino Doucette in a canoe with a salmon that they gave to Len Pratt to land.

PHOTO: MARI HILL HARPUR, 2002 – MHH PERSONAL COLLECTION

would labour over the choice of his fly, and every day he would record this information in his diary. Although his life was involved in business and management, his heart was never far from the woods. He was a lumberman who took his father's timber company (Hampton Affiliates) from a modest beginning into a major entity in timberland ownership and lumber manufacturing. His energy and passion for life shaped the corporate culture at his company's offices in Portland, Oregon. John loved fly-fishing, which he practiced whenever and wherever he could. You might say that John wore his passion for the sport on his fishing vest. He was always willing to help and share his enthusiasm.

∞

Alan Macdougall, a roommate of Doug's from university, recounts:

> One June evening at Hill Camp, Doug and I enjoyed a long night of looking at the beautiful starry sky with a wee bit of single-malt Scotch beside us. We hardly realized the time passing, and of course the darkness of night only lasts a few hours at those latitudes. Before we knew it, the sun was starting to rise. We decided to go trout fishing at Chambers's Falls. During the hike through the bush, there was a great amount of stumbling and staggering, on and off the path to the fishable water. Finally, we positioned ourselves at the river's edge. But not for long! Instantly, I fell into the river up to my neck before I was even able to cast. Eventually, success! We caught two small trout, maybe a pound each, and staggered back to camp for breakfast. All enjoyed our breakfast fish and laughed at our adventure. They were pretty small fish, but they were big for us!
>
> I have so many fond memories of being at camp; like the time when by myself I went wading in Deforest Pool. I was fly-fishing with a dry fly, and the water was quite low. I decided to stage a photograph of myself standing in the middle of the river on the sandbar. I set the timer on a large fallen tree trunk and set the timer. Okay, I had ten seconds to look professional, and I ran to my pre-marked spot and started fly-fishing. I have kept that portrait to this day in a frame on my desk. There are so many great memories: the quiet, the weather, the water and those Zen-like times on the river.

∞

Len Pratt came fishing at Hill Camp in 2002. He did not have any luck catching a fish, but that never bothers a fisherman, and it certainly did not bother Len. He loved the camp life and all the people. On his last day, he was packing his equipment and he returned his rod to the rack before he went to dress for the trip home to Minnesota. Meanwhile, Doug was busy in Len's assigned pool, which was just above the camp. Doug caught a fish! It was a beautiful salmon, and he brought it slowly downriver, past the guides' camp, past the women's camp, and finally to the bottom of the beach steps. By then, Doug's yelling had called all of us out of the house, including Len. "Lenny, I caught your fish. Come on and bring it in!" There was never a more entertaining sight than seeing such a grateful and enthusiastic man, dressed in city clothes and nice shoes, bringing in his fish on the side of the river.

Len, who in 1980 had earned the "Builder's License Number 1" for the state of Minnesota, was as comfortable in the board room as he was on the river, and he is also a wonderful lyricist. After Len came fishing at Hill Camp, in 2002 he wrote this poem, titled "Hill Camp Choir":

> There is a choir that sings
> At the Rivière St-Jean
> Pools and drops
> And flies by name…
>
> Salmon called home
> From seas afar
> Gives "rise" a new refrain
>
> Hill camp magic
> Gives to all who view
> A chance to know a
> Genteel art called… fishing
>
> Whose pace that does inspire
> A depth of thought to currents below
> That somehow hold
> The truth indeed.

∞

Paul Sheeline had recently retired from his position as a director of Pan American World Airways. Although he told his wife she could fly anywhere in the world as long as she stayed in an Inter-

Doug Harpur and Paul Sheeline on the porch, lost in thought.
Photo: Mari Hill Harpur – MHH Personal collection

Continental Hotel (which was owned by Pan Am), he fortunately made an exception to his rule when he came to stay at Hill Camp during numerous visits. In the early 1990s, Paul fished at Hill Camp with Anson Beard Jr. One evening at dinner he told us his story about being eighteen years old and a single man in the armed forces. Paul had volunteered for fieldwork in what was then occupied France. In the dead of night, he reported in at an airfield somewhere in Morocco. There was one plane and its pilot. There wasn't even an extra seat for Paul to sit on, and he had to sit on an oil drum for twenty hours. Paul was in uniform and those clothes were his only possession. He had not thought to bring food or even a Thermos of coffee. During the flight, the pilot gave Paul his sandwich, saying, "Son, I wouldn't change places with you for anything in the world. Here, at least take my sandwich." Paul was dropped behind enemy lines. His mission was to set up the resistance movement in that country. Paul was in the Air Force from 1942 to 1946, and for his successful deployment in that country's underground, he received a Silver Star, the French Legion of Honor, and Croix de guerre with palm for his heroic services. When Paul fished, his full concentration was riveted to the task at hand. His technique was graceful and accurate. He also used to jiggle his little finger on the line just below his reel in order to make the fly move enticingly at the end of the line. It was something he had picked up fishing for trout, and it served him well with the salmon, too.

Tony (Anthony) Smith and Doug discussing their fly box.
PHOTO: MARI HILL HARPUR, 2009 – MHH PERSONAL COLLECTION

Donald Thom instructing Captain Peter Harpur on the finer points of casting, 2010.
PHOTO: MARI HILL HARPUR, 2010 – MHH PERSONAL COLLECTION

∞

Tony (Anthony) Smith and his wife Frances joined Doug and me at Hill Camp in 1986. That fishing season, Doug and I were wondering if Hill Camp life was something we wanted to hold on to, something we wanted to pursue on our own, without my parents' involvement. So, we decided to do a trial run. The resulting week of fishing would be a rehearsal for our future and give us a flavour of running the camp by ourselves. Tony and Frances willingly accepted our invitation, and we are so glad they did.

This was the first time Doug and I organized our own group of friends for a week of fishing. Tony, an entrepreneur and somewhat older than Doug, had been a very strong business mentor for Doug. Fortunately, Tony is an avid and devoted fisherman and conservationist, and is the only fisherman we know who has actually gone to Scotland to take a course in fly-fishing. Having fished on many rivers around the world, Tony maintains that Hill Camp was and is always the highlight of his fishing year. He often refers to the salmon as "the fish of ten thousand casts" because one year he left the camp after three weeks of having caught only one fish, and his arm was nearly paralyzed from casting. On those slow days of fishing he had timed and counted his casts. At the end of that week, I remember Tony saying: "Even though this fish has taken ten thousand casts to catch, I have had a marvelous week! This place is special and should be preserved. Why wouldn't you

hold onto this? Keep the camp running and protect your valuable salmon!" And so we did.

As one of our earliest guests, Tony holds the record for being the guest with the most consecutive fishing years at our camp. In his business career, Tony went on to start one of the earliest Internet companies in the United Kingdom. He has never lost his love of fishing or of the tactile science of that perfectly executed cast.

∞

Donald Thom is among the premier custom-home builders of the Ottawa region. He is also a passionate angler. He is well recognized as the Canadian defender of the World Fly Fishing Championship and received the silver medal in 2009. Donald has represented Canada several times in this capacity. Presently he is coaching the Canadian Youth Fly Fishing Team. Al Macdougall, mentioned previously, remembers one of Donald's fly-casting lessons with Captain Peter Harpur in these words:

When I think of Hill Camp, I cannot leave out the story about Peter receiving his first lesson on catching a salmon in the St. John River. Donald Thom was the instructor, even as he pretended to be a salmon at the end of the line. Both men were standing on the lawn in front of the camp. Peter held the rod and reel while Donald, some thirty feet [nine metres] away was hanging on to the leader [the small filament attached to the fishing line on which a fly is normally knotted]. "Okay?" Donald yelled. "Now drop your line so it is just above the water line, in this case the ground." Donald started running in the opposite direction. He pulled the leader hard to the ground as if he were a salmon who had just taken the fly. "Raise your rod tip and let the line go, raise your rod tip! Let the line go!" Then Donald ran away another fifteen feet [4.5 metres] yelling, "Let the line go, let the line go!" Donald turned and ran twenty feet [6 metres] toward Peter yelling, "Reel in, reel in!" In one quick motion, Donald pulled the line and let it snap upward, yelling again, "The salmon jumped, drop your rod, drop your rod and bow to the king!" Watching Donald on the front lawn of the camp pretending to be the salmon on the end of the line sent us all into gales of laughter. While Peter had the rod and continued fishing, Donald demonstrated how to play the fish. None of us, including Peter, would ever forget that lesson.

Donald was forever remembering and recounting his own versions of his fishing experiences. One evening at dinner, he told us one of his favourite fishing narratives from the St. John River:

> About twenty years ago, the same summer when the big fires were burning about a hundred miles east of Hill Camp, in Forestville, Quebec, I was fishing with Yoland Beaudin. Each evening when we returned to camp after fishing, we could smell its smoke wafting along the river. Because of the hazy sky, the sun was a bright red ball against a dark red and grey background. It was spectacular. We had been fishing in one of the wide-open lower pools, so we had a long way to travel by canoe before we got back to home for dinner. The sky darkened even further with an approaching lightning and thunderstorm. Both of us watched it apprehensively. When the first rumble started, I yelled over the sound of the storm, "No we can't leave yet! The fish are coming! The fish are coming in with the rain. Look at it, Yoland, they are there, right there where the rain starts. The fish will be right in front of the rain!"

To demonstrate his point at the dinner table, Donald picked up his steak knife as if it were a fishing rod. He started casting, gesturing as if he were in the canoe.

> See, I started to false cast just like this, as far as I could: once, twice, more than five times, and I kept going as far as I could reach. Further and further. I wanted to touch the beginning of the rain with my fly.

Continuing to cast with his knife he said:

> I could see the rain approaching and it looked like a wall of water. It was almost a sheet of rain, and my line was almost there. I yelled out, "The fish are right there. Yoland, they are coming. They are coming NOW!" It was just the way I had imagined it. By the time I brought him in, we had a nice twelve-pound salmon.

To this day, Donald and Yoland remember their experience with fondness. Donald could not remember the fly pattern he used, but I have always wondered if it was the old-fashioned feather fly called Thunder and Lightning.

∞

Doug and I went to the Toronto airport, not to take a plane but to introduce ourselves to Tim Wallis, a native of Wanaka, New Zealand and an extraordinary man who had become the world's most respected Red Deer farmer and aviation entrepreneur. Without having seen a photo of Tim, I could pick him out easily. His very

Tim Wallis at the camp door, ready to meet the new day.
PHOTO: MARI HILL HARPUR, 2007 – MHH PERSONAL COLLECTION

presence was tangible. He is tall, and that day wore a pure wool blue sweater. He possessed an easy and inviting manner. The twinkle in his eye was enough to invite my inquiry, "Are you Tim Wallis?" So began our deep and vibrant friendship and fruitful business relationship. Together, we never looked back. Our common interests in farming, forestry and fishing were enough to ignite many an evening conversation.

In 2004 Tim enjoyed fishing at Hill Camp so much that, as a very successful angler, he would catch fish easily and often.

Al Macdougall wrote of his first encounter with Tim in 2007:

> *Hill Camp is an amazing place. A history of a hundred-plus years that reminds you about the past, and just physically being there gives you the feeling of participating in a time of great importance. There, we had the chance to meet so many people from all walks of life. We had the opportunity for friendships and plenty of interesting conversations around the dining table. I have met contractors of the Quebec area, and businessmen from Britain, doctors from the Midwest, and knighted people from New Zealand. One of my favourite memories started with a day with Sir Tim and Lady Prue Wallis on a day trip upriver to 30 Mile Falls while the guides handled the canoes.*
>
> *The three of us went upriver, leaving the camp after breakfast. Nothing stopped Tim, who had been in fifteen helicopter and plane accidents*

Tim Wallis in a specially fitted canoe with guide Yoland Beaudin.
PHOTO: MARI HILL HARPUR – PERSONAL COLLECTION

and had to learn to walk three times and learn to speak twice. Tim, Prue, and I went for the day trip with our lunch in tow. Along the way, we stopped to eat at a sandbar, then we continued on to visit the falls. It was a day trip for us, but the salmon had spent longer swimming to arrive at the same destination. Once there, we saw the place where the salmon went. We saw the big pool where they rested until the water was low enough for them to ascend the substantial incline to arrive

Etsuko and Wye Yoshida.
PHOTO: MARI HILL HARPUR, 2001 – MHH PERSONAL COLLECTION

Flies tied by Denis Blanchette, from top left: Grey Heron, Tiger Ghost, Green Picasse, and a White Wing Picasse.
PHOTO: MARI HILL HARPUR, 2001 – MHH PERSONAL COLLECTION

A wet Green Picasse fly #4 tied by Denis Blanchette.
PHOTO: MARI HILL HARPUR, 2009 – MHH PERSONAL COLLECTION

at their primary spawning grounds above the falls. This was amazing to see. Tim and Prue stayed involved with the entire goings-on and enjoyed the whole tour, as did we him. For Tim, it was difficult to use his legs to get around, but somehow he managed to see everything and be everywhere. Much like those salmon we had come to know, nothing slowed Tim down. Tim was especially at ease when he discovered that his wheelchair fit perfectly in the canoe, as if it were custom made! Persistence and perseverance are the two qualities that have always accompanied this southern man who was born on the West Coast of the South Island. He has had a long journey and still is enjoying his life of an extraordinary seventy-plus years. I will never forget "Formidable Tim." He is an example for all of us.

∞

When Etsuko and Wye Yoshida visited Hill Camp in 2009 they shocked the salmon with their new and unusual flies, with patterns never seen on the St. John. As a child, Wye had been fascinated by the study of entomology. What were these small insects and how had they developed their strong relationship with our ecosystem? In his spare time, he would search out answers to his questions.

Owing to his great-uncle's influence and his own intense passion and curiosity, he was able to master the English language and that, above all, helped him discover the art of fly-fishing. Today he is an accomplished fly caster, master fly-tier, and thoroughly skilful fisher. His fly-fishing career brought him from Japan to North America, where he sought to expand his fishing skills as well as his business acumen. He accomplished both goals. After he retired from his family's group of businesses, dominated by one company, YKK Zippers, he continued to practice the company's philosophy—The Cycle of Goodness—making a practice of the motto: "One prospers when one renders benefit to others." The Yoshida fishing store in Montreal supported and encouraged modern, effective, and ethical fishing practices.

∞

As a final remark on the subject of flies, let us turn to an old friend, John Brown, who was quoted by Daniel Davies in his report: "John Brown gives it as his opinion that the trouble and expense put into flies is all nonsense. He says that one kind of a fly is just as good as another; that often it is well to change the fly; but that a piece of red flannel will do as well as anything else, quite frequently." What angler could dispute the use of variety in the quest to attract attention from the elusive salmon?

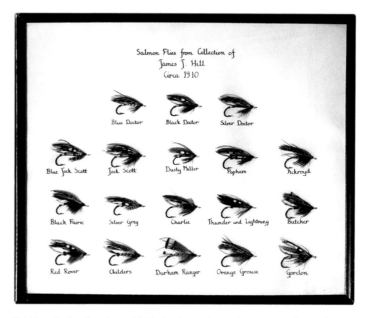

This fly collection from James J. Hill's time has an interesting story attached to it. A few years ago, Jean Chambers came into camp with this framed collection of great-grandfather's flies. Jean had mysteriously received it from someone who wanted to return it to the camp, where they believed it belonged. I did not ask, and Jean did not tell. Who will ever know the reason for the collection's journey? Regardless of its ownership transfer, the gesture was much appreciated by all of us. These are wonderful examples of the older hair-winged flies.

PHOTO: MARI HILL HARPUR – PERSONAL COLLECTION

David and Janet Lines from Bermuda celebrate their 50th wedding anniversary at Hill Camp in 2009.

PHOTO: MARI HILL HARPUR – PERSONAL COLLECTION

∞

In the 2009 season, David and Janet Lines from Bermuda celebrated their fiftieth wedding anniversary at camp. It was a festive occasion, and Janet topped it off by catching a much larger salmon than David had! "I was always the top rod, even in ocean fishing!" Janet exclaimed. David and Janet have fished extensively and offer their time-tried Bermudian advice: "Jumping fish and barking dogs do not bite." And, "Never bring a banana into the canoe as it will bring bad luck."

∞

Dr. Corrin H. Hodgson introduced a Norwegian tradition to Hill Camp: a salute to the morning sun. Corrin fished at Hill Camp on numerous occasions and called his visits to the camp "Fishmas" (a play on "Christmas"). When the fishing was slow, he would assemble us at sunrise on the front porch. He would pour several small glasses of orange juice and float one or two tablespoons of Crown Royal rye on top of the juice. We were instructed to hold our glasses between our thumbs and little fingers and drink the contents down in one gulp. Being thus fortified, we were required to loudly recite the following prayer:

> *Solen er opp, en klar dag,*
> *hanen hilser med ving-slag.*
> *Opp med merken, hen pa verken,*
> *alle som en.*
>
> The Sun is up, a clear day,
> the rooster greets with beating wings.
> Up with the banner, hands to the work.
> All is One.

Corrin would add: "Skol to the salmon. Skol to the guides. Skol to success!"

Corrin attributed this speech to King Olaf Tryggvason. In 1085 AD, the king left his home country of Norway to do great battle with the Swedes at the Battle of Stikklestad. He gathered his troops in the morning mist before sunrise, and he delivered this prayer. This ritual must be performed with the approximate demeanour King Olaf would have affected at the battle, with force and conviction.

Following is another of Corrin's beloved quotations—this one a Sanskrit salutation to the dawn—which he would recite along the riverbank:

∞

"The Scots produced the two most nerve-wracking sports in the world: golf and fly-fishing.

Fortunately they also produced Highland Wine to calm those shattered nerves."

– Discussed at Hill Camp in 1986 by William (Bill) Barclay of Hudson, Quebec

∞

"I've lost my salmon virginity!"

– Shouted by Dr. Gabrielle Slowey after she caught her first salmon on the St. John River

∞

"Fish don't have tongues, and hence they can't gossip."

– Tibetan proverb (Tibetans traditionally detest gossip and they reward the fish for keeping their mouths shut by not eating them.)

∞

James Tieman, a career officer with the Canada's Foreign Service, is seen here reciting and performing the appropriate ritual at Hill Camp in 1992.

PHOTO: MARI HILL HARPUR – MHH PERSONAL COLLECTION

Dr. Corrin Hodgson returning to camp after the evening rise in 1994. Photo: Mari Hill Harpur, 1994 – MHH Personal Collection

Look to this day for it is life;
And in its brief course lie all the variety and realities of your existence.
The bliss of growth, the glory of action, the splendour of beauty;
For yesterday is but a dream, and tomorrow is only a vision.
But this day well lived makes every yesterday a dream of happiness,
And every tomorrow a vision of hope.
Live well, therefore, this day.

Corrin's family originated on the Isle of Man, and he was born in the Midwestern United States. While there he embraced Scandinavian traditions and read, travelled, and fished widely. It would have been at the time he lived in Rochester, Minnesota, that he came across the speech by King Olaf, which he then adapted to his favourite sport of fishing. Sadly, Corrin passed away in 2007, at the age of ninety-eight.

∞

Fisherman's Prayer

I pray that I may live to fish
Until my dying day,
And when it comes to my last cast
Till then I humbly pray:
That when I am in the Lord's great landing net
And peacefully asleep,
That in his Mercy I be judged big enough to keep.
Bow to the King of Fish; bow to Salmo salar.

Acknowledgements

This book would not have been possible without the support and contributions of many individuals and organizations.

Thanks to the helpful people at the Hill Family Papers at the Minnesota Historical Society. Mark Haidet, Eric Mortenson the photo lab supervisor, and Lori Williamson have been particularly diligent and patient in supplying the necessary access, documents, and photographs to both Eileen and me. We are indebted to their fine preservation of so many of my family's documents and mementos.

This text is enhanced by the personal memories of the many anglers who fished the river and by their diligent recordings of their experiences. I would like to especially acknowledge Meredith Alden, who kept a diary of her visits and showed she was a wonderful storyteller in addition to being a fine fisher of salmon.

My family played an impressive role in supplying the support, patience, and content necessary to write this book. I will be forever appreciative of their commitment to seeing this project through to completion. In addition, the private family papers and objects supplied by my family, especially those offered by my cousins Ann and Sheila ffolliott, were incredibly helpful.

My cousin, Anson McCook Beard, contributed numerous anecdotes about life at camp, which he both experienced firsthand and had heard about from his father, who ran the camp successfully for over thirty years. Some of these stories appear in a privately published book entitled *A Life in Full Sail*.

My cousin, Dick Slade, supplied the awesome documentation written sixty years after his first visit to the river. His narrative is humbly accepted into the mosaic of the Hill Camp history in chapter five. Charlie Peet, another cousin, contributed support and donated a version of a film taken by my grandfather at the St. John River. Dick and Charlie have been magnanimous supporters of this history.

Of course, I must salute the local communities along the north shore of the St. Lawrence, and those who have found homes near the St. John River. Many people have for generations lived the lives of fishermen and have supported the fish in a manner that held preservation as a primary goal. I wish to acknowledge their influence on conservation and applaud their efforts to protect the habitat of *Salmo salar*. Jean Chambers, his daughter Joyce, and his sister, Martine Chambers, as well as his extended family, contributed immensely to this book by relating the history of the village of Rivière St-Jean and the chronology of their family. They, along with other locals—the Dérosbys, the Beaudins, the residents of Longue-Pointe-de-Mingan, and the St-Jean Maloneys, among others—have been key players in this story. I appreciate all of these contributors. If there are people I have failed to mention, I apologize for my error.

Our solicitor, Hubert Besnier from Sept-Îles, has kept us going through difficult times and watched over the St. John River as if it were his own. We have called on him during stressful and troubling circumstances, and fortunately we have also enjoyed many fine hours of friendship together. He is a wonderful historian, and his knowledge and passion contributed to the early chapters in this book.

Other contributors who brought their expertise, style, and dedication to the creation of this book, and to whom I am deeply grateful:

- Dr. Fred Whoriskey has made a valuable and outstanding contribution by supplying direction for our St. John River research project. Without Fred, Hill Camp would be ignorant of the wonderful possibilities that have unfolded because of this program, which he has personally directed ever since 1998.
- Walter Scott kindly allowed a copy of his very interesting early Jesuit map of the north shore of the St. Lawrence to appear in this book.
- Ann Mitchell is an artist from North Hatley, Quebec, whose work can be seen in her book *Where the Heart Is*, by Ann Mitchell (Boston Mills Press, 1996). Ann painted the opening illustration in chapter five.
- Elisabeth Skelly is a fine artist and an excellent fisher from Dalkeith, Ontario, who studied at École des beaux-arts in Montreal, Quebec. Her work, which appears on the cover, is a pencil and watercolour study depicting the three stages of a salmon's life.
- B. Guild Gillespie is an illustrator and writer from western Canada. Brenda lives on the British Columbia coast, where she goes by B. Guiled ('beguiled'). She has a BSc in Zoology, an MSc in Environmental Education, and is a life-long, self-taught artist. She has been illustrating fish and shellfish for over thirty years. Her illustration of an adult *Salmo salar* appears on the title page.

- Sandra Gillean, who read and reread portions of this document, kept track of so many details and provided a huge safety blanket in the early days of the project.
- Meaghan Craven, the most conscientious editor imaginable, made professional and thoughtful suggestions and never once faltered in her support.
- Dr. Gabrielle Slowey, professor of Political Science at York University, reviewed an early version of the text and shared her knowledge of the Montagnais peoples in the St. John River region.
- Dr. John Gamble, professor of Geography, Environment, and Earth Sciences at the University of Victoria, reviewed the text on geologic evolution in the area of the St. John River. His suggestions resulted in a clearer account and are appreciated.
- Dr. Ephraim Massey, an emergency medical doctor in the Montreal area, has been a friend and consultant to this manuscript. He has lent his expertise as a fisherman who has visited Hill Camp on several occasions in the 1990s. Ephraim is a fellow writer and helped us to make the copy exact and fluid. His suggestions were extremely welcome.
- Steve Louis of Studio Lézard, Montreal, has patiently worked with all the photographs and completed the layout and design work of this book. He is a pleasure to work with and has made numerous creative contributions both in concept and illustration. Steve is a true friend and a remarkable visual artist.
- Finally, Eileen R. McCormack has become a part of our family through her thorough comprehension of the history of Hill Camp. She has demonstrated a meticulous and competent knowledge and dedication in pursuing our goals in clearly recounting Hill Camp's early history. Eileen has worked for several years on this project and has been fastidiously careful and thoughtful in her approach. She provided constant verifications of the facts and documents that led to our creating an entertaining record of Hill Camp. This book needed Eileen to showcase this story as living history as it unfolded on the north shore of the lower St. Lawrence. It is to you, Eileen, that I take my bow. Thank you from the bottom of my heart for accompanying me on the path of this historical journey. What a wonderful and fulfilling experience it has been!

Three canoes, 1992.

PHOTO: MARI HILL HARPUR –
MHH PERSONAL COLLECTION

Bibliography and a Note on Sources

The James J. Hill and Louis W. Hill Papers in the Hill Family Collection are housed at the Minnesota Historical Society in St. Paul, Minnesota. The author relied on historical data contained in these archives when writing about events from the late 1890s to James J. Hill's death in 1916. The author is grateful for the letters, documents, photographs, maps, and ephemera contained in these collections.

Research for material in chapters five and six that date after 1916, including personal remembrances, letters, documents, photographs, and maps, are derived from the Mari Hill Harpur Personal Collection. The author also made use of a variety of private collections as she researched and wrote the book, including the Meredith Alden Private Collection, Jean Chambers Private Collection, ffolliott Private Family Collection, Walter Scott Private Collection, and Sara Maud Vanier Private Collection.

Additional sources are listed in the bibliography at right.

Bibliography

Anderson, William Ashley. *Angel of Hudson Bay: The True Story of Maud Watt.* Toronto: Clark Irwin, 1961.

Beard, Anson McCook. *A Life in Full Sail.* Privately published, 2011.

Before the Lake was Champlain. DVD. Directed by T. W. Timreck, Peter Frechette, Frederick Wiseman. Wellesley, MA: Hidden Landscapes LLC, 2009.

Bruemmer, Fred. *The Arctic.* Montreal: Optimum Publishing, 1982.

Butterfield, C. W. *History of the Discovery of the Northwest by John Nicolet in 1634 with a Sketch of His Life.* Cincinnati, OH: Robert Clark and Company, 1881.

Carter, George F. "Before Columbus." *Ellsworth American* (November 23, 1990).

Comeau, Napoleon A. *Life and Sport on the North Shore of the Lower St. Lawrence and Gulf.* Quebec: Telegraph Printing Company, 1954.

Left: Line dryer for drying traditional silk lines. After four hours of fishing, the silk lines needed to be removed from the reel and dried.

Right: Rod cases with rods enclosed are made from Indian bamboo, especially the traditional bamboo rods fashioned by the famous Hardy Bros. Ltd., Alnwick, England.

Photos: Mari Hill Harpur, 2013 – From the Private Collection of the River Wye

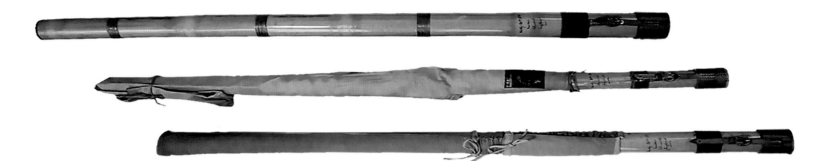

Cooper, Steve. "Coffee with Lefty Kreh." *Fly Life: Australia and New Zealand* 67 (Autumn 2012): http://www.flylife.com.au/library/articles/67/Coffee% 20with%20Lefty%20Kreh.pdf.

Day, Frank. *Here and There in Eramosa: An Historical Sketch of the Early Years, and the People and Events Contributing to the Growth and Development of the Township*. Rockwood, ON: Leaman Printing Company, 1953.

Dérosby, Odette. *Jetons l'ancre sur Rivière Saint Jean 1856 – 1998*. Quebec: 2005.

Dube, Peter. *Stolen Treasure*. Bloomington, IN: Author House, 2009.

Fischer, David Hackett. *Champlain's Dream*. Toronto: Alfred A. Knopf Canada, 2008.

Gilbert, Heather. *Awakening Continent: The Life of Lord Mount Stephen, Volume I*. Aberdeen, Scotland: Aberdeen University Press, 1977.

—. *The End of the Road: The Life of Lord Mount Stephen, Volume II*. Aberdeen, Scotland: Aberdeen University Press, 1977.

Hill, James J. "The Natural Wealth of the Land and its Conservation." Address, conference on the conservation of natural resources, The White House, Washington, DC, May 13 – 15, 1908.

Knox, E.L. "The Tenth Century: Viking Raids." Accessed July 2013. europeanhistory.boisestate.edu/westciv/10thc/11.shtml.

Lockett, Jerry. *Captain James Cook in Atlantic Canada: The Adventurer and Map Maker's Formative Years*. Halifax: Formac Publishing, 2010.

Mitchell, Ann. *Where the Heart Is*. Erin, ON: Boston Mills Press, 1996.

Moorehead, Warren K. "The Red-Paint People of Maine." *American Anthropologist* 15 (January – March 1913): 33 – 47.

The Mystery of the Lost Red Paint People. DVD. Directed by T.W. Timreck and William Goetzmann. New York: Timreck Productions, 1987.

"National Holiday Quebec." Accessed July 2008. en.wikipedia.org/wiki/NationalHoliday.

Parfit, Michael. "Lost at Sea: What's Killing the Great Atlantic Salmon?" *Smithsonian Magazine* (April 2002): http://www.smithsonianmag.com/science-nature/lost-at-sea-1-60417425/.

Reford, Alexander. *Reford Gardens*. Montreal: Quebec Gardens Association, 2001.

Schuster, Angela M.H. "Letter from Newfoundland: Homing in on the Red Paint People." *Archaeology Magazine* 53, no. 3 (May/June 2000): http://archive.archaeology.org/0005/abstracts/letter.html.

Sephton, J. "Saga of Eric the Red 1880." University of Leicester, UK, Distance Learning. Accessed July 2013. sagadb.org/eiriks_saga_rauda.en.

Severin, Timothy. *The Brendan Voyage: A Leather Boat Tracks the Discovery of America by Irish Sailor Saints*. New York: Random House, 2010.

Thomas, Suzanne. "St-Jean-Baptiste Celebrations." *Canadian Encyclopedia*. Accessed July 30, 2008. www.thecanadianencyclopedia.com/en/article/st-jean-baptiste-celebrations.

Trudel, Marcel. "Jacques Cartier." In *Dictionary of Canadian Biography Online*. Accessed October 30, 2007. http://www.biographi.ca/en/bio.php? BioId=34229.

Troubetzkoy, Alexis S. *Arctic Obsession: The Lure of the Far North*. Toronto: Dundurn, 2011.

Weeks, Edward. *The Moisie Salmon Club*. Barre, MA: Barre Publishers, 1971.

Gallery

Mari Hill Harpur on the river's edge.
PHOTO: SARA MAUD VANIER, 2001 – MHH PERSONAL COLLECTION

I always wanted to be an artist, even before I knew what that meant. My family was sympathetic to my dreams, and, the same year I learned to drive a tractor, my parents had a rudimentary darkroom built in a laundry closet in our house. Now, over sixty years later, I still think back to my simple childhood pursuits and wonder at the journey that has led me to illustrating and writing this book about a river in eastern Canada. I am so lucky to be able to share this with you.

The region of the St. John River has always been a source of inspiration for me. The following pages contain a selection of some of my favourite photos.

       – MARI HILL HARPUR

Village of Rivière-St-Jean taken from Robin's Point, 2013.

Seabirds flying along the river, 2013.

Granite outcropping in the St. Lawrence, 2007.

Andrea Holz and Will Slade, 2014.

Woman looking out to the St. Lawrence, 2014.

Boardwalk through the Galets with the
village of Natashquan on the horizon, 1995.

The church in the village of Magpie, 2010.

Evening return to camp, 2008.

Evening lght with three canoes on the beach, 2014.

The distinctive rock formations at the entrance to the 30 Mile Falls, 2001.

Cornus canadensis (dwarf dogwood), 2008.

On the path to Manitou Falls, 2014. These trees are influenced
by the moist microclimate adjoining the Gulf of St. Lawrence,
hence the trees are relatively large and lush.

Guards leaving for their night patrol, 2014.

Pierre and his father, Philippe Piétacho, 1995.

Salmo salar, 2009.

Table set for two, 2012.

Granite rock on the Gulf, 2014.

Tidal Flats, 2014.

Man walking in the forest, 2008.

Pitou the dog, and Robin Chambers, 2012.

The graveyard in the village of Sheldrake, 2012.
The inscriptions face the sea rather than the road.

Full moon over Frigate Pool, June 12, 2014.

"In the end, we will conserve only what we love,
we will love only what we understand,
and we will understand only what we are taught."

— BABA DIOUM
SENEGALESE CONSERVATIONIST, 1968

A group of Atlantic salmon resting below the surface of the Grande River, Percé, Quebec, August 28, 2012.
PHOTO: CHARLES CUSSON, DIRECTOR, QUEBEC PROGRAMS, ATLANTIC SALMON FEDERATION.